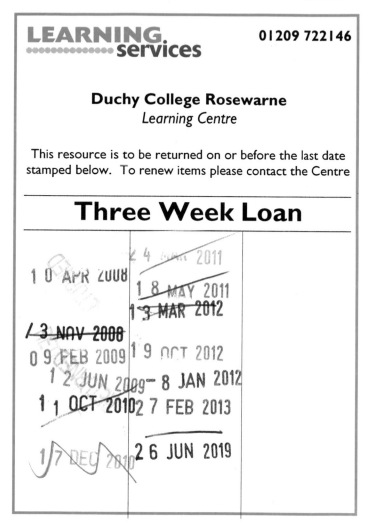

LEARNING services

01209 722146

Duchy College Rosewarne
Learning Centre

This resource is to be returned on or before the last date stamped below. To renew items please contact the Centre

Three Week Loan

1 0 APR 2008	2 4 MAR 2011
	1 8 MAY 2011
	1 3 MAR 2012
1 3 NOV 2008	
0 9 FEB 2009	1 9 OCT 2012
1 2 JUN 2009	- 8 JAN 2012
1 1 OCT 2010	2 7 FEB 2013
1 7 DEC 2010	2 6 JUN 2019

Woodland Management and Conservation

BRITAIN'S ANCIENT WOODLAND

Woodland Management and Conservation

Charles Watkins

DAVID & CHARLES
Newton Abbot   London

ASTROV: . . . (*pointing to the map*) Now look here! It's a picture of
our district as it was fifty years ago. The dark and light green stands for
forest; half of the whole area was covered with forest. Where there is a
network of red over the green, elks and wild goats were common . . . I show
both the flora and fauna here . . . Now look lower down. That's how it was
twenty-five years ago. Already you see, only a third of the area is under
forest. There are no goats left but there are elks . . . And so it goes on.
Let us pass to the third map – a map of the district as it is at present.
There is green here and there, but only in patches; all the elks have gone,
and the swans and the capercailzies too . . . In fact, it's a picture of
gradual and unmistakable degeneration . . .

Chekov, *Uncle Vanya* 1899
(translated by Constance Garnett, Chatto and Windus, 1923)

© Nature Conservancy Council 1990

Photographs by Peter Wakely unless
otherwise acknowledged

**British Library Cataloguing in
Publication Data**
Watkins, Charles
    Woodland management and conservation
    – (Britain's ancient woodland).
    1. Great Britain. Woodlands.
    Conservation & management
    I. Title   II. Series
    333.75'0941

ISBN 0–7153–9329–4

Printed in Great Britain
by Redwood Burn Ltd   Trowbridge
for David & Charles Publishers plc
Brunel House   Newton Abbot   Devon

Contents

Foreword

Ancient woodlands have become part of the vocabulary of the countryside. Whereas in 1970 the ecologists had barely formulated the concept for themselves, by 1990 ancient woods have been debated in the House of Lords, have received special consideration in the national forestry policy, continue to be the subject of successful major appeals by an expanding Woodland Trust and have been explored by major research programmes in ecology, history and forestry. Their ecological importance, and the sense of history and place they impart, has made these remnants of the medieval and prehistoric landscapes a focus for conservation concern.

This interest has come not a moment too soon. Since 1945 the half million hectares of surviving ancient, semi-natural woodland in Britain has been greatly reduced. 10 per cent has been destroyed by clearance, mostly for agriculture; 30 per cent has been changed into plantations, many of them coniferous; 50 per cent has stood unmanaged – only 10 per cent survive under the traditional form of coppice, wood-pasture and high forest management. The Broadleaves Policy, initiated in 1985, may have arrested the clearances and the ingress of pure conifer plantations, but native woodlands are still being replaced by plantations.

Throughout the 1980s, the Nature Conservancy Council has been compiling a national inventory of ancient and semi-natural woodlands, and preparing maps showing the extent of ancient woodland in each county and district. Our inventory has shown that, while about 35,000 ancient woods survive, the great majority are very small. Moreover, most of the larger ancient woods are wholly or partly given over to plantation forestry. Only one ancient wood in ten receives protection as a Site of Special Scientific Interest or is owned by a conservation body. The material from the inventory has been made available to conservation, forestry and land-owning organisations and government agencies, but the lists, maps and data-sheets do not by themselves convey the interest and importance of ancient woods, nor do they indicate how they might be managed. Accordingly, we have complemented our dry and dusty compilation of facts and figures with a trilogy of books under the series title *Britains's Ancient Woodland*.

These books have been made possible by the generous support of ESSO UK plc. For four years they have not only underwritten the work of the two authors, but have helped in many ways with technical advice and publicity. We would like to thank in particular John Peters, Martin Timms and Richard Barister for their support and encouragement.

The three volumes are:

Woodland Heritage by Peter Marren
Woodland Management and Conservation by Charles Watkins
Discovering and Exploring Ancient Woodland by Peter Marren

Each book can be read independently. *Woodland Heritage* is an introduction to ancient woodland history and wildlife, emphasising the unique qualities that make these woods so special. *Woodland Management and Conservation* looks at the ways in which woodland management can be adapted to benefit wildlife. It also offers a do-it-yourself guide on how to find out more about your own local wood. The last volume presents, for the first time, a detailed survey of ancient woodland in Britain, emphasising the local character of our woods, and including a gazetteer of some of the finest woods open to the public. We hope that the publication of these guides will encourage you to explore ancient woodland and to take part in helping to conserve these precious relics of yesteryear.

George Peterken
Peterborough

Introduction

Over the last twenty years our knowledge of the history and ecology of British woodland has been transformed. It is now widely thought that many woods throughout the country are the descendants of the primeval woodland which covered the country before humans started to clear it for agriculture, or manage it for wood and timber. Although the great age of many woods was recognised by some nineteenth-century foresters and ecologists such as J. Main and C. Reid, it is not until the last couple of decades that the subject has received significant attention. This new interest in woodland history has stemmed from the work of historical ecologists, and documentary sources and field evidence have been brought together to show that many woods are of great antiquity. There is also considerable continental interest in ancient woodland.

This book sets out to describe how ancient woods should be managed for the purposes of nature conservation, and is aimed at woodland owners and managers and all those who have an interest in the management and history of such woodland. It does not discuss the technical details of managing woodland: excellent guides are already available (Brooks 1988, Evans 1984, Blyth et al 1988, Hibberd 1988). Neither does it deal in any detail with the cultural aspects of woodland history (Daniels 1988, Thomas 1983).

This book is divided into three parts. In Part I (Chapter 1), the different types of woodland found in Britain are defined and the various categories of ancient woodland are described. The chapter goes on to assess the importance of ancient woodland for nature conservation. Part II (Chapters 2–3) is called 'Finding Out About Ancient Woodland' and the chapters assess critically the huge variety of historical and field evidence which can be drawn upon when investigating the history of ancient woodland. This part of the book can be used, in the first place, to help discover whether any particular wood is ancient. Once this has been ascertained, the sources described in Part II can be used to explore, in more detail, the past management of the wood and the possible effects that this will have had on its current state. As a thorough knowledge of the past management of an ancient wood can be of crucial importance in deciding on the best way of managing that woodland today, this part of the book aims to provide a comprehensive review of the sources available. Chapter 2 deals with published maps, records covering recent woodland management and published historical material. Chapter 3 assesses the value of various unpublished historical records and the use of field evidence.

The management of ancient woodland for nature conservation is examined in Part III (Chapters 4–9). Chapter 4 deals with general management factors which may be relevant for any type of ancient woodland. The treatments each of the main types of ancient woodland should receive for nature conservation are considered in subsequent chapters. Chapter 5 discusses the management of coppice and coppice-with-standards; Chapter 6, broadleaved high forest; Chapter 7, coniferous and mixed high forest and Chapter 8, grazed woodland. At the end of each of these chapters there is a series of management guidelines. Chapter 9 deals, in a similar way, with the management of non-woodland habitat associated with ancient woodland.

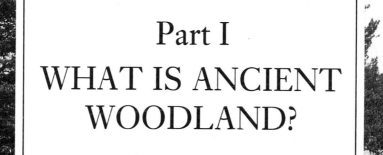

Part I
WHAT IS ANCIENT WOODLAND?

1 The Origin and Value of Ancient Woodland

The Origin of Different Types of Woodland

Although only a tenth of Britain is wooded, there is a tremendous diversity of woodland and the different types need careful definition. Fig 1 shows the origin of different woodland types in diagrammatic form. The original woodland cover may be termed *natural woodland* because it was largely unaffected by human activity. The natural woodland has also been called the *wildwood* (Edlin 1947, Rackham 1976). No natural woodland exists today because all woodland has either been cleared and destroyed, or managed in some way.

Woods which have survived clearance to the present day, and which are remnants of the natural woodland are called *primary*. Although they have been affected by human activity such as the grazing of domesticated animals or coppicing, the site on which they grow has never been ploughed or cultivated.

The long-term trend until the eighteenth century was woodland clearance, but there were periods when land already cleared be-

The origin of different types of woodland, showing the distinction between ancient and recent woodland

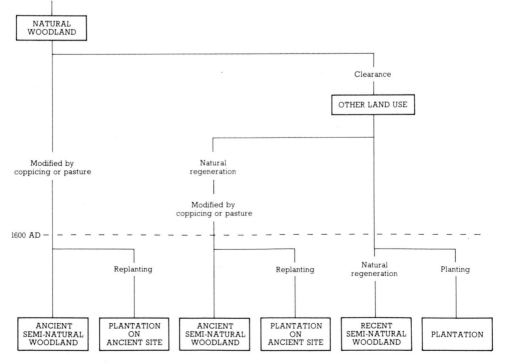

came wooded again. This new woodland, growing on formerly open ground, is known as *secondary woodland*. It results from either the reversion of land to woodland through natural regeneration or the making of plantations.

Natural succession to woodland tends to take place when land falls out of cultivation or when the grazing pressure is reduced. This process occurs in periods of agricultural depression such as in the late nineteenth century. In the present century new secondary woodland has sprung up on abandoned commons, awkward corners in fields, old quarries, disused railway lines and ungrazed and uncultivated chalk downs.

Most modern secondary woodland has been specifically established in the form of *plantations*. Landowners from the late seventeenth century onwards made many new plantations. The landscape of some areas, such as the Dukeries on the poor sandy soils of north Nottinghamshire or the estates of the Dukes of Atholl in Scotland, was completely changed by extensive plantings. Plantations were an essential element of the parks formed by landscapers such as Capability Brown and Humphry Repton, and in addition many small plantings were established as fox and game coverts.

Most secondary woodland today, however, consists of the huge plantations made by the Forestry Commission and the private forestry companies in the uplands and on the lowland heaths since World War I. Modern afforestation is so extensive that most woodland is now secondary and growing in the uplands, while in the early nineteenth century the majority was ancient and growing in the lowlands.

It is very difficult to prove that a wood is primary: the plant and animal communities in the oldest secondary woods have had such a long time to develop that the ecological differences between them and primary woods are relatively insignificant. Secondary woods of more recent origin can, however, be fairly readily identified. They differ from older woods because:

1 they have often grown up or been planted on soils which have been altered by centuries of cultivation;
2 they have often arisen on sites which were isolated from primary woods and so many woodland plants and animals have not been able readily to colonise them;
3 plantations made from the seventeenth century onwards, and especially in the present century, were often made with exotic, introduced tree species, rather than with trees which occurred in the natural woodland.

It is useful to distinguish between *ancient woods* which originated in or before the sixteenth century and *recent woods* which originated from the seventeenth century onwards. All recent woods are by definition secondary; ancient woods, on the other hand, are a mixture of primary woodland and secondary woodland of medieval or earlier origin. The *age* of a wood refers to the length of time which the site has been continuously wooded, not the age of the trees in the wood.

To what extent can any of these different types of woodland be called *natural?* The scattered fragments of primary woods have usually survived because they were an important source of timber and wood. Few, if any, are now natural in the sense that they owe their characteristics entirely to natural processes. They may, however, contain a large number of the tree species, plants and animals which were characteristic of the natural woodland. The natural characteristics of many old woods were recognised by nineteeth-century agriculturalists and foresters. West (1842), for example, made a careful distinction between ancient woods, which were essentially composed of coppice or coppice-with-standards, and plantations. Main (1839) pointed out that remnants of the natural forests remained in some of the royal forests and private parks, and could also be found 'occupying broken or marshy ground, or precipitous slopes inaccessible to the plough.'

At the opposite extreme, there are plantations of exotic trees which are almost entirely artificial. In fact most woods are neither completely natural nor completely artificial, but somewhere in between. The less artificial a wood is, the greater is its interest for nature conservation. Stands which are mainly composed of native trees growing from self-sown seedlings, or from coppice regrowth which itself has originated from self-sown individuals, are termed *semi-natural woodland*.

Unfortunately, the distinction between semi-natural woodland and plantations is a good deal more complicated than it appears at first sight (Savill and Evans 1986). There are several reasons for this. First, stands of native trees which are artificially planted where they could grow naturally increasingly resemble stands of more natural origin as they mature. Second, a stand may be more or less natural in composition, but totally artificial in structure. This is the case with coppiced woodland made up of mixtures of native trees and shrubs. The reverse may also occur. A stand may be artificially composed of exotic species such as sycamore and spruce, yet have a natural type of structure. Third, there is the question as to which trees should be counted as native. Ecologists usually define this in strict terms to include only those species which arrived by natural means and which grow on soils and in regions where they would grow naturally. Thus sycamore is not counted as native but as a long established exotic tree. Moreover, beech planted in Scotland is not counted as native, nor is Scots pine in southern England, although both are native to other parts of Britain. Finally, even where there is no other ambiguity, the self-sown elements within a stand can form any proportion of the growing stock. This can make the classification of planted areas which have been swamped by natural growth very difficult.

As a result of these complications, it may be difficult to determine whether a stand should be classed as semi-natural, or as a plantation. In practice, mature plantations of native trees growing within their natural range are often regarded as semi-natural. Stands which were originally intended as plantations but which have a high proportion of natural growth well beyond the thicket stage may also be classed as semi-natural. Whatever rules are made to decide the matter, borderline cases are bound to occur.

Types of Ancient Woodland

Most ancient woods have survived because they were managed. In general terms, ancient woods were managed either as *coppice* or *wood pasture*. In some upland areas, however, management was less important, and areas of *high forest* have survived.

Coppice is a management system where trees and shrubs are cut at or near ground level, and the next crop grows mainly as shoots from the old stumps. This was only possible where grazing animals were excluded from the freshly cut areas. Coppice was cut at intervals from five to forty years

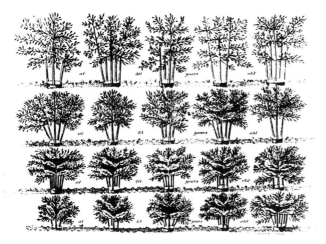

This engraving from Monteath's The Forester's Guide and Profitable Planter *(1824) shows the growth of ash coppice at, 15, 20, 25 and 30 years following cutting*

Coppice-with-standards at Garston Wood, Cranborne Chase in Dorset. The hazel coppice is of poor quality. This is partly due to the relatively closely spaced mature oak standards. The young birch trees to the right of the photograph probably grew up from seed when the coppice was last cut

depending on its growth rate and the use to which the poles and brushwood were to be put. Generally, some trees were spared at each cutting and allowed to grow to a large size. When they were eventually felled, at between sixty and one hundred years old, these *standards* yielded construction timber, bark and firewood. Oak was by far the most commonly grown standard species, but the coppice, or *underwood*, was usually a mixture of species derived from the natural woodland.

From the late eighteenth century onwards there is documentary evidence that the density of stools, ie the roots or stumps of felled trees, in some coppices was increased by the planting of additional trees to be treated as coppice. Usually it was the the most useful native trees such as ash or hazel that were planted. In some parts of the country, and especially in the South East, coppices were planted up with chestnut.

Wood pasture is a system where woodland is permanently used for pasture, with the trees providing both shelter and wood. It was mainly restricted to deer parks, unenclosed forest woods, and commons (see Chapter 8). The trees were often managed by means of *pollarding* which entails the repeated cropping of trees by cutting their branches off at a height above the browsing line. Natural regeneration was confined to periods when grazing was restricted. Established trees, however, often survived for centuries.

(Opposite, above) *Lime coppice at Swanton Novers Wood, Norfolk. This coppice is cut rather higher than normally. Some of the stools are as high as 4ft (1.2m). The stools show a year's young growth. The row of trees in the background form part of the wood hedge*
(Opposite, below) *A stand of mature native Scots pine at Glen Tanar National Nature Reserve, Aberdeenshire. The 35 main remaining areas of native pine woodland cover in broad terms about 12,000 ha (30,000 acres)*

(Above) *A view of part of Windsor Great Park in Berkshire. This shows some of the main elements of wood pasture. The old park oak dominates the scene. In many areas of wood pasture, such oaks were pollarded until the nineteenth century, when the practice gradually died out. In the background, the thorn and birch trees indicate that grazing pressure has been reduced in recent years*

Over the last two hundred years or so, semi-natural woodland has been increasingly replaced with plantations. Although many plantations were made in the eighteenth and nineteenth centuries, little ancient woodland was planted up until the present century. Amphlett (1901), for example, was still able to write that the Wyre Forest in Worcestershire was 'a considerable tract of native woodland which [has] possibly never suffered more at the hand of man than thinning and felling.' By 1900, the market for coppice products had almost collapsed and during the first half of the present century, coppices became increasingly neglected (Collins 1985, 1988; Rackham 1980). At the same time, a national forest policy which depended largely on the planting of even-aged plantations for the rapid growth of timber became established. The way was clear, therefore, for the conversion of much coppice into plantation (Watkins 1984c). Today, in most counties, between 30 and 60 per cent of all the surviving ancient woodland is now classified as plantation, while over the country as a whole, about half the remaining semi-natural woods are neglected and unmanaged (Kirby et al 1984).

The woodland that we have inherited is a complicated mixture of the old and the new; the natural and the artificial. For convenience it can be divided into four classes:

1 Ancient woodland with semi-natural trees and shrubs.
2 Ancient woodland which has been planted up.
3 Recent (after 1600) semi-natural woodland.
4 Recent plantations.

Individual woods may consist solely of one of these types of woodland, or they may be made up of any combination. Ancient semi-natural woods are the most important woods for nature conservation and it is these, together with ancient woodland which has been planted up, which form the subject of this book. Many of the guidelines for the management of ancient woodland for nature conservation, however, are also applicable to recent woodland, especially if it is semi-natural.

The Importance of Ancient Woods for Nature Conservation

Ancient semi-natural woodland includes all the remaining primary woodland in Britain. As primary woods are the direct descendants of the original woodland cover, there is good reason to believe that the species and communities which can be found in them are similar to those which characterised our natural woodland. The tree species may well reflect the natural conditions of the site. Thus within an ancient semi-natural woodland it may be possible to see a mixture of trees made up of sessile oak, small-leaved lime and hazel growing on well-drained sandy soil. In the same wood, towards a valley bottom, there is likely to be a mixture of ash, hazel and alder, while on the waterlogged areas adjoining a stream, alder and sallow might be found. Even if the trees do not reflect the soil changes, the ground flora almost certainly will.

This grading of species according to the soil conditions would also have been observed if it were possible to visit the same area of woodland five thousand years ago. Obviously, the form of the trees would have been different: modern woods rarely have as many large, old trees as their prehistoric predecessors, nor do they have as much dead and rotting timber. The types of species are also unlikely to have escaped some modification. In the original natural forests of Britain there was more lime and wych elm than nowadays and less birch, ash and oak. Nevertheless, primary woods do have a direct link with the original natural forest and, as such, are irreplaceable.

Value for Scientific Research

The link between ancient woods and the natural past makes them very important for scientific research because they can tell us about the natural environment. Oliver Rackham (1980) has reconstructed the range and distribution of natural woodland plant communities by studying the ancient coppices of East Anglia. He has also discovered some of the characteristics of the soils and minor landforms, which appear to have been undisturbed since the last ice age, found in these woods.

Another feature that can be found relatively undisturbed in ancient woods is the pattern of watercourses. If in hydrological studies of lowland Britain, for example, you needed examples of unmodified headwater streams, you would probably have to turn to the streams within ancient woodland. Not only have streams surrounded by farmland prob-

Since World War II many ancient woods have been replanted with conifers. Here at Chaddesley Woods, Worcestershire, an area has been planted up with a mixture of conifers including Thuya plicata. *The dense shade cast by the conifers may be seen in the background. Following the introduction of the Forestry Commission's Broadleaved Woodland policy, such replanting is increasingly rare*

A woodland stream at Glovers Wood in the Weald, on the borders of Surrey and Sussex. Such streams are likely to be much less disturbed than streams outside ancient woodland. The trees include ash coppice and birch. Some of the coppice stools are dying, and the stand will gradually take on the characteristics of high forest unless coppicing is reintroduced. The bank in the background is covered with bluebells

ably been heavily modified and straightened into ditches, but they also drain land which has been ploughed and hence subjected to accelerated erosion.

Ancient woods can also be used to study how woods grow when they are not managed. At Lady Park Wood in the Forest of Dean, for example, mixed coppice has been allowed to grow unmanaged for a century and the woodland is now beginning to acquire a natural structure. Detailed observation starting in 1945 has shown how this type of natural broadleaved woodland behaves and the im-

portance of natural catastrophes, such as the drought of 1976, in shaping the structure of woodland (Peterken and Jones 1987, 1989).

Even those ancient woods which are not primary have considerable value. Dimbleby and Gill (1955) for example, showed that woods that had grown up in late medieval times on heathland in the New Forest still had the podsol soils characteristic of heath. This demonstrates that soil changes caused by woodland clearance are not easy to reverse. Other studies (Rackham 1975) have used secondary woodland adjoining primary woodland to show how long it takes for certain plants to colonise the new woodland.

An important feature of ancient woods is their value as controls in the scientific sense. If we assume that the soils of such woods are relatively unmodified by management, we can use these natural soils as reference points for comparison with the soils of agricultural land and thereby check, for example, the extent to which modern agri-

Fauna and Flora

cultural methods may be degrading soils by altering their structure or stimulating erosion (Collins 1978).

Botanists have long recognised that ancient woods are of particular value because of the species they support. The eminent botanist Druce (1902) noted that in Northamptonshire: 'It is only in the remains of the older woods . . . that any great variety of woodland plants is to be found.' The value of ancient woodland was made more explicit by Ley (1908) who considered that:

> It is mainly to its heirloom of the aboriginal woodland that the rich development of the fruticose Rubi in Herefordshire is due . . . the woodland is extremely rich both in forms and individuals. This fact, when contrasted with the poverty of the planted 'spinneys' of Leicestershire and other English counties, affords a strong pre-sumption that the Herefordshire woods are really aboriginal.

The founding fathers of ecology also recognised the value of ancient woodland. Salisbury and Tansley (1922) noted, when describing the woodlands of the Malvern area that:

> . . . the existing woods largely occupy abrupt slopes and ridges. This distribution, together with the large number and variety of shrubs in the undergrowth, and the occurrence of rare or local herbaceous species are clear indications of descent from primitive forest. There has been a certain amount of local planting, but . . . there is no reason to suppose that . . .

Herb paris (Paris quadrifolia L.) is a species characteristic of ancient woods. It is shade tolerant and is sometimes difficult to find because it frequently grows amongst dense patches of dog's mercury. Herb paris is a poor colonist, and is therefore largely confined to areas of old woodland

Some woodland snails are good indicators of ancient woodland. This snail (Zenobiella subrufescens) *is a local snail found in damp old woodland in Britain and Western Europe* (Photograph by Derek Rands, reproduced by kind permission of the Conchological Society of Great Britain and Ireland)

[this] ... has in any way modified the ground flora.

Ancient woods generally contain a much greater variety of species than recent woods, and they are also far more likely to contain rare and localised species. To quote an example from central Lincolnshire (Peterken and Game 1984), ancient woods over 3ha (7½ acres) in area contained on average one and a half times as many woodland herb species as recent woods of the same size. Rare species, moreover, were much more likely to be found in ancient woods. Thus the twenty rarest species in the area were collectively found in eighty woods and of these woods, 85 per cent were ancient, even though only a quarter of the woods in the area were ancient.

Why do so many species survive in ancient woods? The explanation is complicated but stems from the interrelationship between humans and the native woodland. Woodland once covered almost the whole country. Open ground was found as small, isolated, and in many cases temporary, patches surrounded by woodland. Today, of course, this state of affairs is reversed. The woods are now the small isolated habitats and they are surrounded by large areas of open ground.

Woodland species, however, have not changed. Unlike the species of open and disturbed ground, many woodland species are poor colonists. They tend to be trapped where they grew or lived originally, and rarely make the leap across open ground necessary to colonise new areas of woodland. Some species are so strongly confined to ancient woods that they are known as *ancient woodland indicators*. The value of ancient woodland indicators was recognised at the end of the last century by Reid (1899). He was interested to discover why certain species were local in occurrence, although there were many other sites on which it was just as suitable for them to flourish. He thought that: 'In the altered state of our woods these anomalies are particularly difficult to understand' and suggested that:

some of the difficulties may be cleared up when we have studied each patch of ancient woodland, however small; for by searching small isolated patches of old forest we can often find outliers of the sedentary woodland mollusca and plants, such as probably were once extended over wide areas now bare of cultivation.

This percipient call for a detailed study of ancient woodland unfortunately went almost unheeded for the next seventy years.

Ancient woods are not, however, always clearly and obviously richer in wildlife than recent woods. Indeed in some areas there is little difference to be found between them. Differences will tend to be much less in densely wooded areas, where ancient and recent woods are found close together, and especially where recent woodland grows up adjacent to an ancient wood. Peterken and Game (1981) found that in well-wooded north Northamptonshire, dog's mercury was present in almost all secondary woods of nineteenth-century origin. In contrast, this plant was only present in a fifth of the equivalent woods on similar soils in sparsely wooded west Cambridgeshire.

The type of open land found between woods also has to be taken into consideration. In East Anglia where unwooded ground has long been intensively cultivated, there have been very few opportunities for woodland plants to survive outside woods. In a contrasting area, such as Mid Wales, however, many species characteristic of woods can continue to survive in open ground such as humid, rocky gulleys and streams and under bracken. Here recent woods may grow up on soils that have not been cultivated, and woodland plants may actually already exist on the ground. Thus in the hill districts of northern and western Britain, the ancient woods are not so obviously richer in flowering plants than recent woods, though they are likely to be richer in terms of ferns, mosses, liverworts and lichens.

There are also some areas in the lowlands where ancient woods may be little or no richer in terms of species than recent woods. As one would expect from the discussion earlier, these are mainly the well-wooded districts such as the Chilterns, and districts such as the Weald which have always had a relatively high proportion of uncultivated heath or common land.

In ancient woods we see the original indigenous woodland species. Not all are slow colonists, for some have evolved to take quick advantage of temporary clearings created when large trees fall. Not all are restricted to woodlands: primroses grow happily on cliffs and railway embankments. These opportunistic and adaptable species need little help to survive and can generally be found in recent woods, but the existence of ancient woods is crucial for the survival of the less adaptable species.

As well as being of great value for nature conservation, ancient woods are of historical significance: they often vie with the parish church as the oldest major landscape fea-

Dog's mercury (Mercurialis perennis *L.) is frequently found in ancient woodland. In some parts of the country, such as West Cambridgeshire, it is a fairly good indicator of ancient woodland. In much of the country, however, it is not a good indicator species because it is often found in recent secondary woodland. Dog's mercury flowers from February to April, and often dominates the ground vegetation of woodland*

ture within any parish (Tubbs 1968). The woodland may have been modified by management down the centuries but so too have many churches. Ancient woods, moreover, make a significant contribution to the regional variations characteristic of the British cultural landscape. The woods themselves, together with the associated banks, ditches and other artefacts are ancient monuments.

Part II
FINDING OUT ABOUT ANCIENT WOODLAND

2 Sources for the Study of Ancient Woodland: Published and Recent Records

There is a tremendous range of historical information available for the study of ancient woodland. This material is scattered in a wide range of diverse records. Some *national* sources, such as Ordnance Survey maps, can be used for the study of every wood in Britain, others such as tithe maps (parts of England and Wales) or the Statistical Returns (Scotland) are restricted to various parts of Britain. The availability of *local* records and maps is even more variable and often depends on accidents of history. Consequently, the best sources to start with are Ordnance Survey maps from which a lot of basic information can be gathered. It is then possible to move on to the more specific sources, and see if they can provide any information for the wood or group of woods in question.

Simple information about woods dating back to the beginning of the nineteenth century is usually relatively easy to gather, but for earlier periods records can be patchy. Woodland history books contain many examples of fine old records detailing past woodland management but these have been gathered from record offices across the country, and it would be unwise to expect such excellent woodland records for any particular wood.

The amount of information that can be taken from the different sources is very variable. Some sources, such as old series one-inch Ordnance Survey maps, will tend simply to show whether the wood existed at the date the map was surveyed, and whether it has changed in shape or size. Other sources, such as some estate records, may provide detailed information about the type of trees found in the wood, and the way in which they were managed.

Records were not made with the modern woodland historian in mind and are often difficult to interpret. Moreover, the quality and accuracy of the sources varies. Because of this variability, it is important to use as many different sources as possible in order to obtain independent corroboration. In addition, map and documentary sources should be used in conjunction with evidence gathered by field surveys of the woodland in question (see Chapter 3).

A number of general guides to historical sources are available, and most of these include useful material for woodland managers and owners. Excellent guides for English and Welsh sources have been written by Stephens (1981) and Riden (1983, 1987), while Scottish sources have been covered by Moody (1986). Invaluable general works include Darby (1973) and the volumes of the *Cambridge Agrarian History of England and Wales*. No discussion of the study of woodland history in Britain would be complete without stressing the importance of the works of Oliver Rackham (1975, 1976, 1980, 1986a and b, 1989). His books are powerful evidence for the value of using a wide variety of sources for the study of woodland history. Other books with useful discussions on sources for woodland history include Anderson (1967) for Scotland; Linnard (1982) for Wales; Peterken (1981); Hart (1966); James (1981); Sheail (1980) and Young (1979).

In this chapter, the sources are discussed under three main headings: first, published maps; second, records dealing with recent woodland management and third, published historical sources. Unpublished historical sources and field evidence are assessed in Chapter 3.

Published Maps
Ordnance Survey Maps

Whether you wish to study the history of a particular wood, changes in the area and number of woods in a parish, or the distribution of woodland in a county, the first sources to be consulted are the Ordnance Survey (OS) maps of the area concerned. OS maps have been published in a bewildering number of editions and revisions at a number of different scales since the beginning of the nineteenth century. The marshalling of successive editions of maps in order to be able to assess woodland change can be a formidable task. Various guides to the general value of these maps for landscape historians explain some of the pitfalls to be avoided (Harley 1964, 1979, Coppock 1968). OS maps are also very useful as base maps on which to note information from other sources. Crown Copyright on OS maps lasts for fifty years so any map older than that can be freely photocopied with the permission of the owner.

Whatever scale of map is used, it is always the *date of survey* that indicates when the woodland was surveyed and not the date of publication or printing. The date of survey is usually given on the map. The situation is confused when maps are partially revised. In some revisions, only 'major changes' such as new roads or housing estates, are shown on the map. Some problems of interpretation are more subtle: revisions of the 25-inch County Series after 1919, for example, only showed change in woodland type for woods over 4ha (10 acres), and changes in smaller woods were ignored.

OS one-inch maps

The first OS maps were produced at a scale of 1in to the mile (1:63,630) and this scale went through seven editions before it was superseded by the metric 1:50,000 series in the seventies. The first maps were published between 1805 and 1840 and covered the whole of Wales and southern and central England. They were based on surveys started in 1784 which had usually been made at a scale of 2in to the mile. These one-inch maps have been called the 'least accurate Ordnance Survey maps' (Coppock 1968) and are often very difficult to date accurately. Similar maps for the rest of Britain were published between 1840 and 1873 for England, 1856 and 1887 for Scotland. After the 1890s the one-inch maps were revised independently of the larger scale maps.

Copies of the old series one-inch Ordnance Survey can usually be consulted in county, city, or regional libraries, or local authority record offices. The reprints of one-inch maps surveyed in the nineteenth century published by David & Charles can also be used, although these are not necessarily the earliest edition. One problem in using these maps is that in hilly areas the engraved marks, known as hachures, which were used to denote slopes, obscure the woodland symbols. A new set of reprints of these maps is being published in ten volumes by Harry Margary (Lympne Castle, Kent), and five volumes of maps covering southern and central England have already appeared.

For most parts of the country it is easy to see from a quick comparison of an old series map and a modern map whether a particular wood was present in the early nineteenth century. In a few areas, however, especially if there has been a lot of recent afforestation or building, it may take some time to locate the site concerned on the map because so many identifiable features have been lost or changed. The old series one-inch maps are a very useful means of discovering quickly whether there was a wood on a particular site when the maps were surveyed. Some sheets distinguish between coniferous and broadleaved woodland, but this is not true for the whole country. They are used as one of the basic sources for the NCC's Ancient Woodland Inventory (Kirby et al

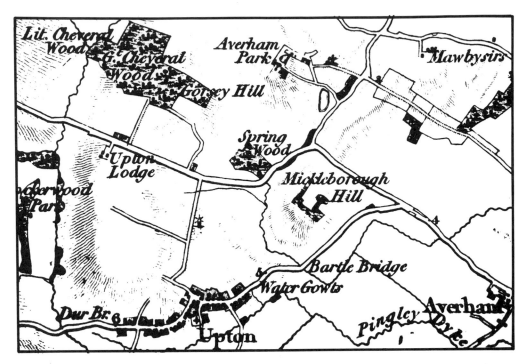

Extract from the first edition of the Ordnance Survey one-inch to the mile map. This shows an enlarged portion of Sheet 70, which covers parts of Nottinghamshire and Lincolnshire. Both Spring Wood, in the centre of the extract, and Great Cheveral Wood are ancient woods. The map was published at the Tower of London on 1 March 1824. Note that slopes are indicated by hachures. In very hilly areas, this can make these maps difficult to read (Photograph by Mervyn Evans)

1984). The provisional inventories contain 1:50,000 maps showing all the ancient woods over 2ha (5 acres) in area and whether they have recently been replanted or still contain semi-natural vegetation.

Comparisons of successive editions of one-inch maps should indicate whether a site has been continuously wooded over the past 150 or so years, and whether it has remained the same shape. Later editions of the one-inch map show whether a wood is coniferous, deciduous or mixed, and the changes shown on these maps can, with caution, be used to give a quick, superficial, history of the woodland types.

There are, as always, difficulties of interpretation. What happened, for example, if a wood was surveyed at the time it was felled? If a wood was coniferous, surveyors were instructed to ask the landowner or agent whether the area was to be replanted, and marked down the woodland type accordingly. In the case of recently felled broadleaved woodland, where the trees and shrubs were naturally regenerating or regrowing from stools, the surveyor could either show the area as wood, or as scattered trees on rough pasture (Harley 1979). Rough pasture could include areas of 'heather, bracken, close growing woodrush or mosses . . . brambles, etc.' (OS, *Red Book*). This explains why it is often possible to discover parts of ancient woods, especially on maps surveyed soon after World War I, shown as rough grazing and not woodland. It also shows how it would be wrong to interpret this 'change' as woodland loss or gain.

OS 25-inch maps, six-inch maps and two-and-a-half-inch maps

It was decided in 1856 that the most useful large scale national survey would be at the scale of 25in to the mile. Most of Britain, apart from uncultivated moorland areas, was eventually surveyed at this scale, and sheets were published for the greater part of the country. Six-inch maps were made for the whole country. These were specially surveyed in uncultivated areas, such as the Highlands, but elsewhere were reductions of the 25-inch survey. The two-and-a-half-inch maps were not introduced until much later, after World War II, but were derived from the basic 25-inch survey material.

The three scales have different advantages and disadvantages for the study of woodland history. The 25-inch maps contain most information, but are often cumbersome to handle: even a small wood can be on four separate sheets. The six-inch map is easier to use, and in its modern guise as the OS 1:10,000 series is the usual base map for woodland management plans and surveys. The two-and-a-half-inch maps are useful for assessing woodland change at the county level, and form one of the time-horizons used in the NCC's ancient woodland inventory.

The first editions of the 25- and six-inch maps were surveyed between 1853 and 1896 for England and Wales, and 1854 and 1895 for Scotland. The detailed methods of survey and classification of types of woodland are difficult to ascertain, because they were constantly being modified over the period of survey. Many of the instructions for surveyors have, moreover, been destroyed. Woods had to be 0.1ha (¼ acre) in area in order to be recorded in the survey. The great advantage of the 25-inch maps over the other scales, is that individual parcels of land are numbered

Extract from the Ordnance Survey 25-inch to the mile map. This is sheet XXX No 13, of the County Series for Nottinghamshire, and is dated 1920. However, the map was originally surveyed in 1883, and revised in 1915. The extract, which is reduced in scale, shows Spring Wood, which is also shown in the map opposite. A tremendous amount of information can be gathered from maps of this scale. A quick glance shows that at the time of survey the wood was 15.560 acres in extent. It had three rides, and adjoins a parish boundary and road. The wood was predominantly broadleaved, but the presence of a scatter of coniferous symbols may be an indication that there was some replanting in the nineteenth century (Photograph by Mervyn Evans)

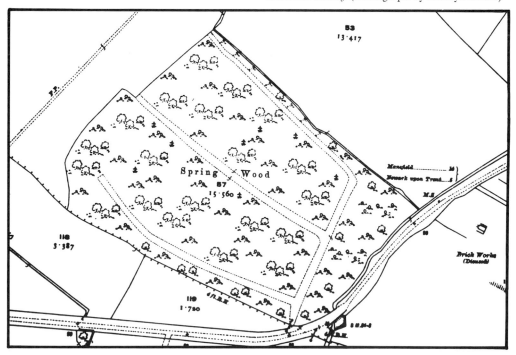

and have their area given in acres. Areas of woodland were almost always separately numbered and given an acreage. Unfortunately, however, the parcels of land delineated may bear little relation to management units, such as coppice falls, within a wood.

OS woodland classification

The vegetation classification used on the large-scale maps was devised in 1855, and although there were many changes of detail, the basic outline remained the same until 1963. The reasons for classifying woodland were varied. Woodland is a prominent landscape feature, and there were therefore important military reasons why woodland type should be clearly distinguished on the maps. It was also necessary to distinguish between timber and underwood, as these were treated differently for tax and rating purposes. As might be expected, the classification of woodland produced to satisfy these military and fiscal demands bore little relation to any ecological classification. Furthermore, as the nineteenth century progressed, less and less vegetation detail was incorporated in the maps. Nevertheless, the 25-inch maps, and in a reduced form the six-inch maps, do hold an enormous amount of woodland information which can be of great interest for the study of the past management of woodland (Wheeler 1984). It is ironic that such a detailed national survey of woodland was being undertaken at the very time traditional woodland management was in decline.

The terminology used to describe the different types of woodland on these maps is sometimes ambiguous. Broadleaved trees were classed as 'forest trees', or 'hard wood'; coniferous trees as 'fir' or 'plantation'. 'Mixed wood' was a mixture of coniferous and broadleaved trees. It is particularly unfortunate from the point of view of ancient woodland that the terminology associated with coppice woodland is so confusing. Three terms: 'underwood', 'brushwood' and 'coppice' seem to have been used interchangeably, although 'brushwood'

has the connotation of patches or clumps of bushes.

How accurate was the classification of woodland on these maps? The instructions to surveyors concerning mixed wood give some clues:

Although the character of woods need not be minutely shown, yet their general character should be truthfully shown. For instance, a fir wood should not be described as 'mixed' wood because it has a few forest trees on its margin; nor a large wood of forest trees be shown as 'mixed' because it has a small clump of firs in one corner. In such cases the general character of the wood will be written [on the survey map], and a few of the special trees will be sketched approximately where they occur on the ground (Johnston 1905, quoted by Harley 1979).

However, the information collected in the field was not moved to the final map in one operation: it was transformed in the different stages of the map-making process. There are therefore likely to be variations from sheet to sheet in the way woodland was represented. This is illustrated by the way that woodland type sometimes changes suddenly at sheet boundaries although the adjoining sheets were surveyed at the same time. One way of carrying out an independent check on the accuracy of the OS classification at a local level would be to compare the woodland type shown on OS maps with that given by estate maps and wood books of a similar date. This would only be possible for estates where suitable records existed, and where the estate maps were original surveys and not adapted from earlier surveys. Prominent and isolated trees were precisely surveyed and placed in their exact position on the map. Most trees, and certainly trees in woods, however, were placed on the map to give an impression of the types of woodland rather than to indicate actual positions: the instructions to draughtsmen for 1906 were that 'trees in a large wood should be artistically grouped and not crowded together' (Harley 1979). Main rides were shown on the maps, but temporary cart tracks and clearings were not.

From time to time, changes in the mapping conventions were made. Before 1880, for example, birch trees were distinguished by a separate symbol, but after that date they were shown by the standard deciduous symbol. This type of modification might falsely give the impression to those comparing successive editions of maps that a change in woodland type had occurred. The history of the birch symbol also demonstrates the care needed when interpreting woodland information at different scales. It was used on 25-inch maps, and on the six-inch maps derived from them, but it was not used on the six-inch maps which were especially surveyed for uncultivated moorland areas. As a general rule, the amount of vegetation detail shown on these maps declined from 1880 onwards. One exception to this is that by the 1880s the distinction between close, medium and open tree cover had been adopted. These distinctions were symbolised by the grouping of tree symbols, but unfortunately, the exact threshold values used to classify the openness of woodland are not known.

Woodland information shown on the 25-inch and six-inch maps is very similar. After 1881 the six-inch maps (apart from those for upland areas) were made by direct reduction from the 25-inch maps so that woodland detail is identical at both scales, although clearer to interpret at the larger scale. Between 1851 and 1881, however, the reduction process involved the re-engraving of the woodland detail with smaller symbols for the six-inch maps. This meant that there was room for error in the transcription of information, although research has yet to be carried out to investigate the relative accuracy of the two scales in this respect.

Eighteenth- and Early Nineteenth-century County Maps
Various maps drawn at a scale of 1 or 2in to the mile were published for most coun-

ties of England, Wales and Scotland during the eighteenth and early nineteenth centuries. These are known as county maps and should not be confused with the 'County Series' of the OS large-scale maps or the earlier small-scale county maps by surveyors such as Saxton or Speed (Harley 1969, Rodger 1972). They provide a useful additional source which can be used in conjunction with the early one-inch OS maps.

County maps are variable in quality, but the broad distribution of woodland is usually correct. The shapes of parcels of land and woods are often generalised, and it is quite difficult to know whether the changes indicated by a comparison of maps of different dates are merely changes in a 'paper landscape' due to different standards of cartography, or ones that actually took place on the ground. This is the sort of problem that can only be solved by a detailed field survey of the wood and surrounding landscape. The date of survey given on the map should be treated with caution, as material from earlier surveys was often incorporated in the map (Coppock 1968). County maps of the early to mid-eighteenth century are particularly useful in determining woods which are likely to be ancient as they were surveyed before the 'plantation movement' really got under way.

Contextual Information from OS and County Maps
The most straightforward information that can be gathered about woodland from maps includes a wood's site, shape and name at the date of survey. This information need not only be taken at face value; it can with experience be interpreted to give clues about the wood's history. Although none of this information can be taken as conclusive evidence that a wood is ancient it may provide useful back-up evidence. The *site* of a wood is important in this respect. Woods near the edge of a parish, or on steep slopes, are more likely to be ancient than woods in the centre of parishes, or woods on fertile and relatively flat land.

Wood *shape* is also useful evidence. Plantations that have been made on new sites from the eighteenth century onwards tend to have straight boundaries. Ancient woods in contrast usually have irregular boundaries. This broad distinction is sometimes upset, however, by the straightening of ancient woodland boundaries through woodland clearance or planting; by the development of recent semi-natural woodland with uneven boundaries; or by the making of irregularly shaped plantations in a conscious effort to fit them into the landscape.

Plantations with irregular boundaries are often important components of landscape parks around country houses, and are becoming increasingly common in the afforested areas of upland Britain (Price 1810, Crowe 1978). Woodland shape can also be

considered in the context of the shape of surrounding parcels of land. In areas which were enclosed from the eighteenth century onwards, the straight lines of the hedge and fence lines will contrast with the irregularly curved boundary of ancient woodland. Plantations, on the other hand, will tend to fit in neatly with the enclosure pattern.

Woodland *names* provide useful hints about the origin of some woods but, again, need careful interpretation. Names tend to change over the centuries, and some blocks of woodland are made up of a number of separately named woods. The term 'plantation' can usually be taken to refer to recent woodland, though sometimes areas of ancient woodland are renamed as plantations if they are replanted. Other names which frequently refer to recent woodland are: 'belt'; 'covert'; 'furze'; 'spinney' or 'stripe'. Names which often indicate ancient woodland are: 'coppice'; 'copse'; 'grove'; 'hanger'; 'holt'; 'park' and 'shaw'. Woods named after their parish are also often ancient. The Ordnance Survey (1987) has published a good introduction to the more common Gaelic and Welsh place names. The study of place names and landscape history is discussed by Gelling (1984).

Recent Woodland Management

Once a woodland has been identified as being of ancient origin, it may be useful to enquire further into the history of the wood. In conservation terms, the recent history of the wood, covering say the last eighty years, can be of crucial importance as it is over this period that old management systems are

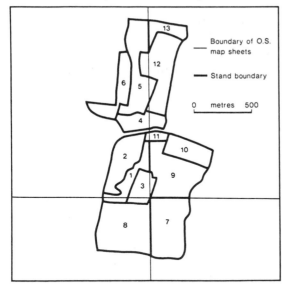

Boundary of O.S. map sheets

Stand boundary

0   metres   500

Stand no.	Area (acres)	Woodland type	Tree species (% of canopy)
1	6	Coppice with standards	70% ash, 20% oak, 10% birch
2	14	Devastated	70% ash, 30% oak
3	6	Coppice	100% ash
4	7	Devastated	40% ash, 30% oak, 20% elm, 10% birch
5	17	Coppice	40% ash, 40% hazel, 20% elm
6	9	Broadleaved high forest	50% oak, 20% ash, 20% beech, 10% birch/elm
7	21	Scrub	spp. present: oak, ash, birch and hazel
8	24	Scrub	spp. present: oak, ash, birch and hazel
9	17	Coppice with standards	50% ash, 30% birch, 20% oak
10	8	Coppice	100% birch
11	2	Scrub	spp. present: oak, ash
12	18	Coppice with standards	50% oak, 40% hazel, 10% birch
13	4	Coppice	40% ash, 40% hazel, 20% elm

Information from the Forestry Commission 1947/9 Census of Woodlands for Eaton and Gamston Woods near Retford in north Nottinghamshire. This plan shows how the wood was divided up into stands by the Forestry Commission surveyors of the time, and the range of information on woodland type and tree species that can be obtained from the original census returns. Both of these woods are now owned and managed by the Nottinghamshire Trust for Nature Conservation (Watkins 1984 a) likely to have decayed and new systems been introduced. In addition to the successive editions of the OS maps which have already been discussed, Forestry Commission censuses, modern estate records and aerial photographs are very useful sources.

Forestry Commission Censuses

Woodland censuses were carried out by the Forestry Commission in 1924, 1947–9, 1965–7 and 1979–82. A census was also started in 1938, but was left incomplete owing to the war. Of the four complete censuses, it is only the second that is of real interest to the woodland historian. The records for the 1924 census have been destroyed, while the two most recent censuses were sample surveys. The 1947–9 census involved a field survey of all woods over 2ha (5 acres) in area not held by the Forestry Commission. The records sheets and maps for England and Wales are preserved in the Public Record Office at Kew; those for Scotland are at West Register House (Scottish Record Office), Edinburgh. Additional copies for separate conservancies were retained by the Forestry Commission.

The woods were divided into stands for the purposes of description, and for each stand information was collected on woodland type, age class, quality of tree stems and percentage stocking. Stands were also assessed as to their suitability for economic management with regard to access, shape and area. Perhaps the most useful information in the census is the proportion of each stand made up of different tree species. Each stand was numbered, and the outlines of the stands were drawn on OS six-inch County Series base maps.

There are some problems involved in using the census records. The information was collected by foresters for silvicultural purposes and not for use as an historical record. Tree species considered important for forestry were more carefully noted than some native species which were commercially unimportant. Surveyors found it difficult to know how to classify overgrown coppice. One of the surveyors commented that:

... we met with considerable areas of that bugbear of Census Surveyors, derelict coppice-with-standards, which has to be classed as either 'coppice-with-standards', 'broadleaved-high-forest' (with scrub undergrowth) or 'scrub' (with scattered standards). This annoying kind of woodland was met with all too frequently ... (Fergusson 1949).

Another problem is that as the census was made just after the war, very large areas had recently been felled, and for these there is no information about woodland type or species. Moreover, the records for woodland which was managed by the Forestry Commission at the time of the census no longer exist. Even though these problems sometimes make the census records difficult to interpret, the 1947–9 census is useful for assessing twentieth-century woodland change (Watkins 1984a). For many woods it helps to bridge the gap between current surveys and any estate surveys which may survive from the nineteenth century.

Modern Forestry Estate Records

Woodland owners who receive grant aid from the Forestry Commission are usually required to manage their woodland to a plan of operations which is approved by the Forestry Commission (Hibberd 1986). Estates which received grants under the dedication scheme from 1948 onwards kept detailed maps showing the date areas were planted, felling dates, areas left unplanted and so forth. In addition some estates keep independent woodland record books and maps. These maps can be a very useful means of discovering which areas have been subject to different kinds of commercial management over the past forty years. They also show what species it was intended should grow in a particular stand.

When such records are compared with a current field survey it is sometimes found that the trees growing in a stand are not the species shown on the map. This may happen in ancient woodland where vigorous coppice regrowth has overwhelmed planted species. If treated with care, however, these records can be an invaluable means of discovering the recent management history of a wood. Because they are working documents, they are usually still held by the owner. Copies of records associated with Forestry Commission grants are held by the Conservancy office, and these may be consulted with the owner's permission.

Forestry Commission Records

These provide information comparable to that found in private estate records but relate to the Forestry Commission's own property. When Forestry Commission woods are sold the new owners should acquire as many of the associated old management records as possible. Again, the records sometimes show the species that were intended to form the final crop in a stand, rather than the actual species present.

An additional group of Forestry Commission records that supply information for woods not managed to a plan of operation are those associated with felling licences. It is theoretically possible to check the records held by the Forestry Commission to see whether any trees have been felled in a wood since World War II. This assumes that the volume of timber felled was high enough to come under the regulations, that if this was so, the owner did not fell the trees illegally, and that the records have been retained by the Forestry Commission Conservancy concerned.

Aerial Photographs

The commonest type of aerial photograph is black and white vertical at a scale of about 1:10,000, that is, roughly 6in to the mile. Although clouds sometimes obscure parts of the landscape, it is usually possible to identify areas of woodland on these photographs. It is also possible with practice to distinguish between conifers and broadleaved trees on the basis of crown shape, shadows and texture.

Tree species are not usually identifiable on this type of photograph (Fleming 1981).

The most readily available sets of photographs for any county are held by the county council. Most counties will have at least one complete set for their area, and some will have a sequence taken at perhaps every decade. In addition, many areas of the country were flown by the RAF and the Luftwaffe in the forties. These photographs can be very useful for assessing post-war woodland change. A central register of aerial photographs is kept by the Ordnance Survey at Southampton (0703 792584). The main English collection is held by the Royal Commission on the Historical Monuments of England, London (01 973 3000). The equivalent for Wales is held by the Central Register of Air Photographs for Wales, Welsh Office, Crown Offices, Cathays Park, Cardiff CF1 3NQ (0222 823815). Scottish aerial photographs are kept by the Scottish Development Department, New St Andrews House, St James Centre, Edinburgh EH1 3FZ (031 556 8400). The Luftwaffe collection of photographs of much of southern and eastern Britain is held by the National Archives in Washington DC (Rackham 1986a). Other important collections are held by Hunting Aerofilms of Borehamwood (01 207 0666) and Cambridge University (0223 334578).

If it is possible to arrange for large-scale aerial photographs to be taken of a particular wood, then these can be very useful. Large-scale colour photographs may be used to identify different tree species and woodland types. If a succession of photographs is taken in the spring, it will often be possible to identify the distribution of different species as they come into leaf.

Landscape Photographs

It is usually a matter of luck as to whether any old photographs which may have been taken of a particular wood survive. Woods are only likely to have been regularly photographed if they were of historic or picturesque value, or if they could be seen from a famous view-

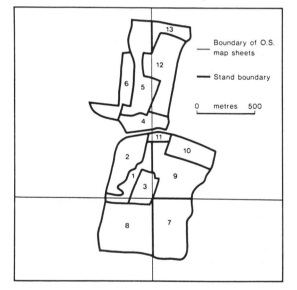

Boundary of O.S. map sheets

Wistman's Wood on Dartmoor has been the subject of
a detailed historical analysis through the use of landscape photographs. The gnarled oaks have long been a
tourist attraction on Dartmoor, and many photographs
exist from the late nineteenth century onwards. The
analysis was made possible because the exact location
of most photographs could be deduced from the shape
and position of the large boulders (Proctor, Spooner
and Spooner 1980)

point. A very interesting study of Wistman's Wood on Dartmoor was able to make extensive use of photographic evidence to show how the wood developed since 1889 (Proctor, Spooner and Spooner 1980). This was possible because the wood is a famous landmark which had been regularly photographed over a long period by tourists and botanists. One difficulty with using photographs for studying woodland change and management is that it is difficult to locate accurately where the photograph was taken. The Wistman's Wood study was able to get round this problem because the wood is growing amongst identifiable large boulders. For most woods site identification is a much more difficult, and often impossible, task.

Collections of photographs taken by some individual photographers and photographic firms can also be useful sources. Good examples are the fully catalogued collection of the thousands of Scottish landscape photographs taken by Alasdair Alpin MacGregor between the wars held by the National Museum of

Woodland information may be discovered from a wide range of photographs. Four cart horses dominate this picture taken outside The Vine Tap in New Street, Ledbury, Herefordshire. The horses are pulling a waggon loaded up with coppice poles. This is interesting, as it is evidence that coppicing was still practised in the area in 1943, the date the photograph was taken (Photograph Copyright National Monuments Record)

Scotland or the late Victorian photographs in the George Washington Wilson collection held by Aberdeen University Library (Taylor 1982). Many recently published collections of Victorian and Edwardian photographs contain examples showing woodland crafts and such photographs provide a vivid impression of working conditions and techniques in the woods. Old postcards can also provide much information (Peterken 1981). Large collections of old photographs are held by the Museum of English Rural Life at Reading University (0734 875123), by the Welsh Folk Museum at St Fagans, Cardiff (0222 569441) and by the Scottish Ethnological

Archive at the National Museum of Scotland (031 225 7531).

Oral History

One source of information that is easily overlooked is the recollections of people who used to manage or work in the woods. They may be able to give information about when the coppice was last felled, or who used to own the wood. Unfortunately, it is notoriously easy to forget dates and confuse the past, and so information from such sources should, if possible, be checked against other data. On the other hand, no other sources are likely to provide details about working practices such as the tools used, the means of extracting timber and poles, local uses of produce, sources of planting stock and so forth. A written record or transcription should be made of any information obtained orally.

Published Historical Sources

Once the recent history of an ancient wood has been investigated, it is likely that its earlier history will need to be considered. Relatively accessible published sources held by the reference and local history sections of libraries should be studied before getting involved in detailed research. The most useful published sources are outlined in this section.

The Land Utilisation Survey Monographs

This survey of land use was carried out between 1931 and 1941, although most of the fieldwork was completed in the early thirties (Stamp 1948). Land use was mapped on OS six-inch sheets and then transferred for publication on one-inch base maps. Many of the manuscript six-inch sheets survive in the library of the London School of Economics. Woodland was recorded as high forest, coppice, scrub or cut-over land, but this information was not included on the published maps. Nor was it tabulated in the ninety-one LUS county monographs which were published between 1937 and 1940. Some of these monographs do contain, however, informa-

tion about the distribution of woodland at the county scale and often include references to articles on woodland history which might otherwise be difficult to track down. Some of them, such as the report for Lanarkshire, contain maps of the distribution of woodland in the late eighteenth century which are based on contemporary county maps.

Victoria County Histories

The Victoria History of the Counties of England is a long-term project established over eighty years ago to produce detailed county histories. Many of the histories for individual counties are incomplete (Pugh 1970). Thirty of the Victoria County Histories contain chapters on forestry. These accounts mainly date from the Edwardian period. Most were written by the historian the Rev J. C. Cox but some were written by a forester, John Nisbet. They contain general information on forestry in the county, especially for the nineteenth century. These volumes also contain chapters on the botany of the counties, and translations of the Domesday Book.

Board of Agriculture Reports

The *General Views* provide a description of the agriculture of Britain around 1800 on a county basis. Many of them contain information of the woodland management for the period, although the amount of detail varies considerably. Some of this information, especially that dealing with plantations and forestry, has been abstracted by Jones (1961) for England and Linnard (1972) for Wales. Anderson (1967) made extensive use of the Scottish *General Views* in his work on Scottish forest history and a list of the Scottish volumes and their authors is given by Symon (1959). There are usually two reports for each county, the first short 'quarto' edition published between 1793–6 and the second, larger and more informative 'octavo' edition often by a different writer, between 1800 and 1817 (Grigg 1967). Not always accurate, these reports tend to be imbued with the contemporary ethos of agricultural im-

(119)

Letter to Sir R. Sutton, Bart.

Warsop, Feb. 4, 1794.

HON. SIR,

THE following are the accounts of Mr. KNIGHT's wood at WARSOP in this county:

Names.	Extent.	
Collyer Spring,	75 ACR.	A spring wood, with fine growing oaks, underwood, as hop poles, &c.
Lord Stubbin	37 ditto	A spring wood as above, but the oaks not so thriving.
Coppice	26 do.	A spring wood, much as last.
Parson Spring	12½ do.	A spring wood, with growing oaks and underwood, as above.
Rough Wood	7½ do.	A spring wood, as above, but the oaks not so thriving.
MosscarrRoughWood	2½ do.	A spring wood, much the same as last.

KIRKTON, *in this County:*

Norton wood,	8 ACRES.	A spring wood, with fine growing oaks, underwood, as hop poles, &c.
Thorney Wood,	8 ACRES.	A spring and timber wood, with very fine growing oaks, &c. What I mean by timber, some part of this wood is rather strong growing oaks, and thick upon the ground.

WILLOWBY, *near Kirton, in this County:*

High Spring,	4 ACRES.	A spring wood, with fine growing oaks, underwood, &c.

Yesterday I delivered your inclosed letter at Mr. ROBINSON's house myself, but he was not home. If, Sir, you want any further account or explanation, I shall be glad to render you every service in my power. And I am, Sir,

Your very humble servant,

SAMUEL JACKSON.

Extract from Robert Lowe's General View of the Agriculture of the County of Nottinghamshire. *Published in 1798, this book contains a detailed list of the woods and plantations of Nottinghamshire in the late eighteenth century. The author obtained information by writing to the agents of the principal estates. This extract provides information on nine 'spring' or coppice woods in the county. Note that one of the principal uses for coppice poles in this area was for hop poles*

provement, which in woodland terms took the form of new plantations. At their best, however, they provide an invaluable account of the woodland management of a county. The *General View of the Agriculture of the County of Nottinghamshire*, by Robert Lowe (1798), for example, provides detailed information on planting techniques; lists of woods and plantations for the different regions of the county and for different owners; the size of the main woods; and notes on the management of coppice woodlands, including yield, rotation, value and species. Much of this information would either be impossible to discover from unpublished sources, or could only be obtained after a long search of estate archives. It is therefore always worth consulting the *General Views* before undertaking detailed research on a wood. Even if the particular wood is not mentioned, it is useful to understand how other woods in the county were managed.

Articles in Journals

The study of woodland history is carried out in many disciplines, and as a result papers are scattered in a wide variety of historical, ecological, geographical, agricultural, forestry and local history journals. Unfortunately, there is no abstract journal which covers the whole range. Although the number of woods which have books or pamphlets all to themselves is increasing, it is unlikely that you would find information about a specific ancient wood published in journals. Sometimes, indeed, individual woods do figure, as in the case of Way's (1913) study of the ownership history of Leigh Woods (Bristol). More commonly, there will be general articles on the woodland of a region or county which can help to provide an understanding of the historical management of woodland in the area.

Local history journals may contain general woodland histories for a county. The older articles, such as those by Robinson (1925) on Herefordshire, Grundy (1939) on Wiltshire or Hedley (1950) on Northumberland tend to concentrate on the history of forests rather than woodland. In recent years, however, articles such as Barton's (1979) on Hertfordshire have tended to concentrate more on the history of woodland management. Other important local research is available in general collections dealing with local history (Henderson 1935) or in locally published booklets (Jones and Jones 1985).

Historical journals from time to time publish articles on wood-using industries, such as the charcoal iron industry (Hammersley 1973); bark peeling and tanning (Babb 1980) and charcoal burning (Linnard 1987). The *Local Historian* includes articles on the use of historical sources and Jones (1984) deals specifically with woodland. Geographical journals such as the *Journal of Historical Geography* include studies of woodland industries (Lindsay 1975) and of the value of particular sources (Watkins 1984a). There is also a considerable literature on woodland clearance (Brandon 1969, Darby 1951).

Forestry journals such as *Forestry*, the *Quarterly Journal of Forestry* and *Scottish Forestry*, often contain articles on woodland history (Roden 1968; Jones 1961; Tittensor 1970) and *Forestry* publishes useful articles on the forestry of different parts of the country (Beaver 1974; Tilney-Bassett 1988). Some of the early numbers of journals founded in the nineteenth century, such as the *Quarterly Journal of Forestry*, the *Journal of the Royal Agricultural Society* and the *Transactions of the Highland and Agricultural Society* contain contemporary accounts of woodland management. The short-lived *Journal of Forestry and Estates Management* which was published from 1877 to 1886 is also a valuable source.

Old Published Forestry and Woodland Management Books

From the seventeenth century onwards a wide range of books dealing with woodland management has been published. A list of over two hundred of these books dealing largely with English works is given by James (1981). Other bibliographies include that in Rackham (1980) and, for Scotland, Anderson (1967). Old forestry books must be treated with caution, they may describe how the author considers woodland should be managed, rather than how it was managed at the time. Others seem to have been written to drum up consultancy work for the foresters who wrote them, in which case there may have been a tendency to exaggerate how badly woods were managed by other foresters.

Nevertheless, some of these books, such

ARBORETUM ET FRUTICETUM BRITANNICUM;

OR,

THE TREES AND SHRUBS OF BRITAIN,

Native and Foreign, Hardy and Half-Hardy,

PICTORIALLY AND BOTANICALLY DELINEATED,

AND SCIENTIFICALLY AND POPULARLY DESCRIBED;

WITH

THEIR PROPAGATION, CULTURE, MANAGEMENT,

AND USES IN THE ARTS, IN USEFUL AND ORNAMENTAL PLANTATIONS, AND IN

LANDSCAPE-GARDENING;

PRECEDED BY A HISTORICAL AND GEOGRAPHICAL OUTLINE OF THE TREES AND SHRUBS OF TEMPERATE CLIMATES THROUGHOUT THE WORLD.

BY J. C. LOUDON, F.L. & H.S. &c.

AUTHOR OF THE ENCYCLOPÆDIAS OF GARDENING AND OF AGRICULTURE.

IN EIGHT VOLUMES:

FOUR OF LETTERPRESS, ILLUSTRATED BY ABOVE 2500 ENGRAVINGS; AND FOUR OF OCTAVO AND QUARTO PLATES.

VOL. I.

HISTORY, GEOGRAPHY, AND SCIENCE; AND DESCRIPTIONS, FROM RANUNCULACEÆ TO STAPHYLEACEÆ, P. 494., INCLUSIVE.

SECOND EDITION.

LONDON:

HENRY G. BOHN, YORK STREET, COVENT GARDEN. 1854.

Title page of the second edition of J. C. Loudon's Arboretum et Fruticetum Britannicum *published in 1854. This work contains a vast amount of information about native and introduced trees and their management*

as J. West's *Remarks on the management, or rather, the mis-management, of woods, plantations, and hedgerow timber* (1842) and R. Monteath's *The forester's guide and profitable planter* (1824) are based on a lot of practical management experience and can give an insight into how woodland managers dealt with their woods and provide essential background information. In addition to the management books, there are two encyclopaedic works which contain an enormous amount of diverse information about trees and woodlands. These are J. C. Loudon's *Arboretum et Fruticetum Britannicum* (1838) and H. J. Elwes and A. H. Henry's *The Trees of Great Britain and Ireland* (1906–13).

County Directories

These are the quickest way to obtain land-ownership details from about the 1850s to the 1930s, and a comprehensive list and guide to their use has recently been published in G. Shaw and A. Tipper's *British Directories*. Directories usually contain a list of the main proprietors for each parish. If the parish is, as was frequently the case, all owned by one person, then this information will indicate who owned the woods in the parish. Where there was more than one owner, it will at least provide an indication as to who might have owned the woodland in question, and enable search in the record office for records associated with the possible owners. It should be remembered that most woodland in the period covered by the directories will not have been let out to tenant farmers, even though their farmland might entirely surround individual woods.

Directories also provide information about the number of people employed in trades associated with woodland produce, and they can be used when trying to reconstruct the local woodland economy of an area (Rackham 1980). They are easier to use, though probably less accurate, than the original returns of the Census of Population which provide more detailed employment information.

Newspaper Advertisments

Coppice and timber sales were often advertised in local newspapers and these advertisements provide information about past woodland management. They are, in general, a much underused source, although M. L. Anderson made extensive use of advertisements appearing in the *Edinburgh Advertiser* in his assessment of the exploitation of Scottish woodland in the eighteenth and nineteenth centuries. The value of this source is shown by the fact that for the period from 1790 to 1804, 118 offers appeared of copse wood for sale. The advertisements also provide information on the methods of extracting timber and the markets for which the produce was destined.

3   Sources for the Study of Ancient Woodland: Unpublished Historical Records and Field Evidence

Unpublished Historical Sources: England and Wales

A wealth of unpublished information can be used for the study of woodland history. To find out whether a wood existed before the appearance of detailed county maps in the eighteenth century, it is usually necessary to consider a wide variety of local records. If there is not enough time for the woodland manager or owner to go into the subject in any depth, it may be possible to persuade a local historian that the history of the wood is worth investigating. Scottish records are rather different to those for the rest of Britain owing to the separate administrative and judicial systems. They are considered on p48.

The quality of information available depends on who owned and managed the woodland in the past. If the wood was always part of a small property, it is unlikely that detailed management records were ever kept. If, on the other hand, the wood was part of a large estate, then detailed records and maps may have been made at the time and used as working estate documents. These can show the types of woodland; amount of timber and coppice sold; dates when timber and coppice was felled; purchasers of woodland produce; amount of money received for goods sold and so forth.

Records are available for some of the medieval religious estates for the early medieval period, and they become fairly common for private estates from the mid-sixteenth century onwards. Most private estate records are written in English, but the writing and spelling may present difficulties. In contrast, court records, including manorial court records, were kept in Latin until the early eighteenth century. From 1750 onwards documents are usually much easier to read, although some handwriting still presents difficulties.

If medieval and later records were kept for a particular wood, where would those records be found today? Some may be impossible to find: they could have been destroyed by fire or water, or simply been lost. If they survive, they could be held by the present or previous owners of the wood. Records referring to royal forests or to woodland owned by the Office of Woods are held in the Public Record Office. Where the wood was part of a large estate which still survives, the records may be fairly easy to locate if they are kept in the estate office or muniment room. If the estate no longer exists, then the records could be held in a solicitor's or land agent's office anywhere in the country. Such records can take a very long time to trace.

In many cases, however, private estate records have been given or lent to the various county record offices and are available for inspection there. An additional problem is that many landowners own, or used to own, estates in different parts of the country. The records for the whole group of estates might have been held at one location, and this can mean that records for an estate in, say, Yorkshire are held by the county record office for Surrey. This problem is quite common in Wales where there was a high proportion of absentee English land ownership.

The Public Record Office

The Public Record Office (PRO) is the central repository for public records and holds an enormous amount of material of relevance to the study of ancient woodland. The documents are indexed under the body they came from. In general, the records of medieval central government and of the law courts are held at the office in Chancery Lane, while those of modern departments of state are held at Ruskin Avenue, Kew. It is always worth phoning the PRO before your first visit to check that the records required are available, and at which office they are held.

The PRO has a 'forestry' category and the reference numbers for all records in this category start with F. Records dealing with the Forest of Dean, for example, are referenced as F3, while F17 contains a series of forest maps and drawings covering the period 1608–1943. Records with woodland information are also found under many other headings, and include: records of the Land Revenue Record Office such as documents, maps and plans of forest lands, parks and estates held by the Crown Estate Commissioners covering the period 1560–1953 (LRRO 1) and twenty-four volumes of Office of Woods letterbooks for 1803–1901 (LRRO

6); records of the Crown Estate Commissioners and their predecessors such as the documents of the Commission of Enquiry into the woods, forests and land revenues of the Crown 1786–93 (CRES 40); and records associated with tithe commutation (IR 18).

County Record Offices and Libraries

County record offices and county, city or borough libraries contain an enormous amount of material which is of importance for the study of ancient woodland. Some woodland records are also held as part of the large collection of farm and estate records at the Museum of English Rural Life at Reading. Record offices vary in size and many have little space, it is prudent, therefore, to make an appointment before calling. Staff at record offices are very helpful and the first step should be to discuss requirements with them.

Material is usually indexed by parish and it is important to know which parish or parishes the wood is in. Go through the index cards for the parish and see if there is any reference to the wood concerned. Sometimes, a general or subject index will contain entries explicitly for woodland, forestry, trees, timber or wood, or all five, and these are also worth checking. If they do not contain information about your

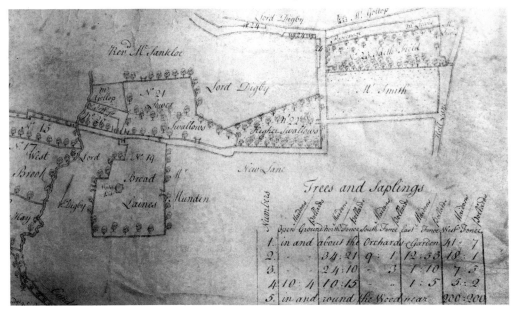

wood, they may contain general information relating to woodland management in the area. Such indexes are usually incomplete and so the lack of reference to say, coppice, cannot be taken as meaning that there are no records on that subject.

If the wood was at any time part of a large estate, it is essential to check whether any of the family and estate records for that property are held in the office. Many such collections of estate records have detailed indexes which have been compiled for the National Register of Archives which is part of the Royal Commission on Historical Manuscripts. Copies of these reports are held by record offices and libraries and a complete set is held at the offices of the National Register of Archives at Quality Court, Chancery Lane. These family records are made up of a mixture of papers including deeds, personal letters and documents dealing with the management of the estate. The records for individual families are usually kept together and so it will be necessary to go through the index volume dealing with the family that once owned the wood, checking for references to woodland. Sometimes, woodland is not mentioned in the index to the family papers. This does not necessarily mean that there are no relevant woodland records; they may simply not have been indexed separately and it is still worth going in detail through the estate management papers looking for woodland documents.

Estate Papers

Maps

Estate maps are usually indexed separately in the estate index as maps and plans. General estate maps can be used to assess the location of a single wood within the context of the estate as a whole. Maps were commissioned

Part of a plan of Candle Marsh Farm, Dorset, by Samuel Donne, drawn in 1765. This very detailed plan shows the number of all trees and saplings growing in the hedgerows and woods on the farm (Reproduced by kind permission of Dorset Record Office: Sherborne Castle Archive, DI KG 2770)

by the owners of estates from the late sixteenth century until the 1870s when accurate large-scale Ordnance Survey maps became available (Harley 1967). As with other records, estate maps should be interpreted with care. They may, for example, be based on earlier surveys, or simply be inaccurately surveyed. Usually individual parcels of land are numbered or lettered on the map and the tenants of the different pieces are shown on an accompanying 'terrier' or schedule of parcels of land. As woods were usually kept 'in hand' and not let out to tenants, maps of the whole estate can be rather disappointing as sources for the study of woodlands. Often only the outline of a wood and its name are shown. This shows that a wood existed, but gives little idea of management history.

Apart from general estate maps, there are also specific maps of the woods themselves. This is particularly true of woods which were coppiced. Such maps are very important means of determining how woods were managed in the past. They often show the boundaries of the areas cut each year, and can be used to work out the coppice cycle for the wood concerned. They also show the pattern of rides and can show ponds, brooks or other features of interest. Sometimes, maps of the wood at different dates survive and it is then possible to discover if the boundaries of the coppice falls, or the ride pattern, have changed over the period concerned. Wood maps can also be used to find out if a wood has remained the same size over a long period, or if it has been partially cleared, or extended. Maps of ancient woodlands rarely show the tree species present and in this respect they differ from estate maps of plantations.

Wood books

Many estates in the eighteenth and nineteenth centuries kept their wood accounts in bound wood books, though sometimes they were simply jotted down on loose sheets of paper. This type of record contains a lot of information on past management, especially on estates where sections of coppice

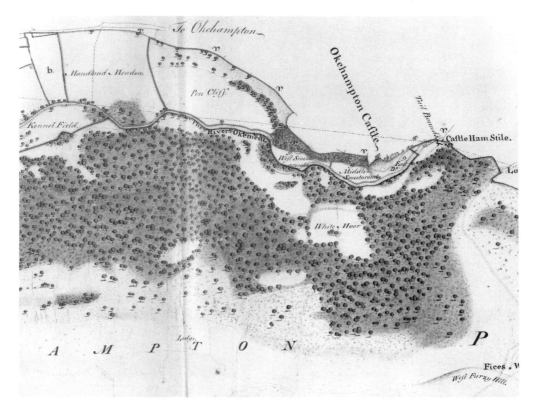

woodland were sold yearly by auction to specialist wood dealers or woodmen. For each wood it was normal to list the separate coppice falls down the left-hand side of the page. They are identified by names, numbers or letters, or combinations of these methods. The next column shows the area of the falls, usually in acres, roods and perches. The following columns usually indicate the years in which the fall was sold and the price it fetched.

For some estates, it is quite possible to reconstruct the coppice rotation of a wood over a period of one or two hundred years. Records of sales of timber were usually kept separately from sales of coppice and include timber growing in hedges and parks as well as woodland. The names and addresses of purchasers of coppice, timber and bark are often given and, if used in conjunction with county directories, it is possible to discover who was buying different woodland produce and for what it was being used.

Part of a plan of Okehampton Park by George Lang, drawn in 1780. The wood is on the northern edge of Dartmoor, and has no definite boundary; rather the trees gradually thin out towards the moor (Reproduced by kind permission of Lord Courtenay and Devon County Record Office)

Miscellaneous records

There may be references to woodland in other estate records. These can give colour to what might otherwise be a rather dull set of essentially economic records. The forester or agent may have kept a diary which gives details about the management that was carried out at different times of the year. There may be letters from the landowner to the agent directing him to fell certain trees, or to retain others because of their landscape value. Every so often, perhaps when an estate passed to a new owner or if there was a dispute over ownership, a surveyor will have been brought in to assess the value of the woodlands. If the surveyor's report survives it gives a valuable description of the estate woodlands at that date.

Game books provide an indication of how intensively the woodlands were managed for pheasants. Deeds do not normally give information about woodland management but are a means of tracking down ownership. Management practices may, however, be implied in the clauses of leases. Such clauses might, for example, restrict the amount of grazing, or the number of trees that should be felled. As with other types of record, the fact that a lease clause states that something should not happen cannot be taken as proof that it did not do so.

Tithe Surveys

The documents and maps associated with tithe reform in the 1830s and 1840s are a rich source of information. The recent publication of two detailed works, upon which this account is based, has made them a much easier source to use (Kain and Prince 1985; Kain 1986). Tithes were from early medieval times onwards the heaviest direct tax on farming. Not all tithes were payable to the church: many had become private property as a result of the dissolution of the monasteries and could be bought, sold and leased at will. Methods of tithing woodland varied from one part of the country to another. In some areas all woodlands were exempt while in others certain species of tree were exempt. Generally speaking, coppice was subject to tithes but timber trees were not.

Extract from A Survey and Account of the Trees growing in Brinscombe Coppice belonging to Brinscombe Farm within the Parish of Corfe Castle within the County of Dorset. *This survey made on 5 and 6 May 1751 provides an estimate of the value of the bark and timber of each tree in the wood* (Reproduced by kind permission of Dorset Record Office: Ryder of Rempstone Archive D86/E38)

The 1836 Tithe Commutation Act was passed in order to convert all remaining tithes, whether paid in cash or in kind, in England and Wales into an annual tithe rent-charge. Tithe commissioners were appointed and they assessed the rent-charge for 11,800 tithe districts, which were usually based on parishes or townships. These tithe districts covered about three-quarters of England and Wales. The areas not dealt with by the tithe commissioners are largely those which had been enclosed by Act of Parliament in the late eighteenth and early nineteenth centuries and which had had their tithes commuted under the Enclosure Act. Once the tithe rent-charge was agreed, it was apportioned over the parish by the tithe commissioners. Most of the apportionment was carried out in the late 1830s and 1840s.

There are three main types of tithe record: tithe maps, tithe apportionments and tithe files. Copies of these documents are held at the Public Record Office at Kew. Copies of the maps and apportionments for many districts are also held by county record offices. Many of the maps were freshly surveyed for the tithe commissioners, but some were redrawn from earlier surveys. Many of those specially surveyed are at the scale of 3 chains to 1in (26.7in to 1 mile).

The maps are by no means perfect sources for reconstructing the former extent of all woodland because many woods consisting solely of timber trees were not subject to tithes and might be omitted from the maps. The maps usually distinguished between plantation, wood and coppice, although these terms were interpreted differently in different places. For broad studies of woodland distribution, therefore, Ordnance Survey maps, or old county maps are often better sources.

The tithe maps should be used in conjunction with the apportionments. They include a schedule in which each separate parcel of land numbered on the tithe map is listed under the name of its owner and occupier. This is one way of finding out about woodland ownership. The schedule also lists the area of each plot and its 'state of cultivation'. It is sometimes possible to find a single parcel where the state of cultivation is noted as 'wood and pasture' or 'wood and arable'. This does not usually mean that these uses are combined on the piece of land rather that two plots of land with distinct uses are parcelled together.

The 'state of cultivation' column information, when used with the name of the parcel, can provide evidence of woodland change. Many parcels of land bearing wood names are recorded in state of cultivation columns as arable or pasture and, conversely, some parcels named as fields are recorded as being used for plantations, coppices or woods. Other hints of woodland change can be deduced from the remarks the commissioners sometimes wrote on the schedule. These might include comments on the grubbing up of trees or the making of new plantations.

In addition to the tithe maps and apportionments, much information was kept in tithe files for each district, although the amount and quality is variable. Kain (1986) has produced a complete index of the information in these files by both subject and place and this should be consulted first. The information about trees and woodland is indexed under six headings: hedgerow timber; coppice; plantations; woodland management; productive woodland; and poor woodland. Tables 1 and 2 show the number of tithe files which contain woodland information by county. A quick glance shows that for many counties, such as Yorkshire, there is hardly any information, while for others, such as Devon and Norfolk, there is a great deal. For coppice woodland, the frequency of cutting is often given and the local tithe agents sometimes provided an estimate of the quality of the tithable woodland. In addition, the species of trees growing in hedgerows were often noted. Kain's index will tell you immediately whether the tithe file for a particular parish or township holds

Table 1 Woodland information in the English tithe files (including Monmouthshire) at the PRO

county	Number of files with woodland information					
	A	B	C	D	E	F
Bedfordshire	–	3	6	–	3	2
Berkshire	3	13	12	1	2	2
Buckinghamshire	1	1	2	4	2	–
Cambridgeshire	–	5	11	–	–	1
Cheshire	–	–	4	–	–	–
Cornwall	88	25	12	1	1	6
Cumberland	–	–	3	–	1	–
Derbyshire	1	1	9	2	1	3
Devon	215	63	31	15	2	2
Dorset	130	64	24	–	–	–
Durham	–	–	1	–	–	1
Essex	–	34	10	–	11	12
Gloucestershire	112	15	9	–	3	2
Hampshire	4	12	13	5	11	24
Herefordshire	165	21	5	1	12	1
Hertfordshire	4	7	5	–	11	13
Huntingdonshire	–	2	1	–	2	4
Kent	–	1	3	2	30	23
Lancashire	1	1	3	–	–	–
Leicestershire	1	–	6	1	–	3
Lincolnshire	2	8	31	2	6	16
Middlesex	1	1	2	–	–	1
Monmouthshire	70	14	–	–	3	3
Norfolk	–	33	68	8	15	92
Northamptonshire	1	3	5	11	2	4
Northumberland	–	–	11	–	–	1
Nottinghamshire	–	3	7	3	1	3
Oxfordshire	–	5	1	–	3	4
Rutland	–	–	–	–	–	–
Shropshire	–	6	19	3	2	1
Somerset	230	68	66	2	8	9
Staffordshire	–	1	7	–	2	3
Suffolk	2	36	41	2	13	21
Surrey	2	6	11	3	4	3
Sussex	1	14	6	–	26	15
Warwickshire	1	2	6	10	6	2
Westmorland	1	1	–	–	1	–
Wiltshire	132	74	9	–	–	2
Worcestershire	82	21	2	–	1	2
Y East Riding	–	–	2	–	–	1
Y North Riding	–	1	5	–	1	1
Y West Riding	–	–	3	–	–	–

A hedgerow timber; *B* coppice; *C* plantation;
D woodland management; *E* productive woodland;
F poor woodland

(abstracted from Kain, 1986, pp562–631)

Table 2 Woodland information in the Welsh tithe files (excluding Monmouthshire) at the PRO

county	Number of files with woodland information					
	A	B	C	D	E	F
Anglesey	12	–	10	1	–	–
Brecon	23	–	4	–	2	1
Caernarvonshire	19	–	17	–	2	–
Cardiganshire	18	2	1	2	1	–
Carmarthenshire	40	2	–	–	–	–
Denbighshire	87	2	17	–	2	–
Flintshire	24	1	7	–	–	–
Glamorgan	25	–	–	–	–	–
Merionethshire	22	–	5	–	–	1
Montgomeryshire	55	2	19	1	–	–
Pembrokeshire	48	1	3	–	–	1
Radnorshire	28	5	–	–	–	–

A hedgerow timber; *B* coppice; *C* plantation; *D* woodland management; *E* productive woodland; *F* poor woodland   (abstracted from Kain, 1986, pp631–42)

any of this woodland information. These files can provide information on the value of coppice woodlands in different parts of the country, although the figures have to be interpreted with care as the value of timber was sometimes included with that of the coppice.

Enclosure Maps and Awards

Enclosure in the eighteenth and nineteenth centuries took two main forms. First, there was the extension of improved farmland by enclosing common land between the freeholders of a parish. This was most widespread in the upland counties where large areas of unenclosed moorland had survived, but could also include commons and areas of old royal forest in the lowlands, such as Needwood Forest in Staffordshire (Nicholls 1972). Second, there was the rearrangement of existing arable and meadow land so that the basic unit of management was the enclosed field rather than the unenclosed strip of land in an open field. This type of enclosure was most important in mid and eastern England where the greatest proportion of parishes with open fields was to be found. From about 1750 until the 1830s, enclosure was normally brought about by an act of parliament. The full details of this procedure are explained by Turner (1980) and Tate (1978). The enclosure documents are in some ways similar to tithe records. The maps show the boundaries of parcels of land and the outline of woodlands, while the accompanying award provides information about land ownership.

The maps do not give any detail about the woodlands or the type of vegetation and can only be used to show that a particular wood existed at a particular time. They are an important source, however, because they provide pre-Ordnance Survey large-scale map evidence for many areas not covered by tithe maps: tithes were usually commuted during parliamentary enclosure and so areas enclosed by this means did not need to have their tithes specially commuted under the 1836 Act. Sometimes parliamentary enclosure involved the clearing of woodland: in three Nottinghamshire parishes in the 1790s, for example, Robert Lowe (1798) noted that 345 ha (850 acres) of coppice was allotted and converted to farmland.

Medieval Records

Oliver Rackham's books provide many detailed examples of the use of medieval records for the study of woodland history (1976, 1980, 1986a, 1989). For many English parishes little survives from before the mid-sixteenth century and Welsh records are extremely rare. What does survive is written in Latin. Some of the most useful records deal with the estates owned by religious houses, the Crown and colleges. The records of Glastonbury Abbey, for example, indicate the management of alder groves for fuel on the Somerset Levels in the mid-thirteenth century (Williams 1970); the Rufford Abbey and Blyth Priory records show how woodland was being cleared in medieval Nottinghamshire (Holdsworth 1972, 1974; Timson 1973), while the records of the Bishopric of Ely include a detailed thirteenth-century survey of its estate including much information about woodland (Rackham 1976).

Many of these records have been translated and published by county historical societies. Manorial extents and surveys provide information about land holdings in a manor and can give details about woodlands. Early estate accounts give information on the income and expenses of individual estates. They may have details about woodland management and also the costs of timber used as building material.

Further information can be deduced from medieval leases and deeds (Alcock 1986), while manorial court rolls may record offences and disputes concerning woodland management. The 1279 Hundred Rolls, which were an enquiry into royal rights collected on the basis of hundreds, provide information on the extent of estates but woods may be under-recorded as only woodland which was in the separate use and possession of an individual is recorded. Unfortunately, the information contained in the Hundred Rolls varies from county to county. The fullest returns are for a group of counties in the Midlands (Harley 1961).

Domesday Book

This 900-year-old document records one of the most complete surveys of land use that has ever been carried out. It was written in Latin but translations are usually given in the Victoria County Histories and have also recently been published by Phillimores of Chichester. The Domesday survey does not cover Wales (but includes a few areas within its modern border) or Scotland nor the most northern counties of England. For each county, the original returns of the survey were grouped together and listed by landowner. If the lands of a village were in more than one ownership, therefore, the relevant survey information is likely to be under a number of separate headings in the Domesday Book.

The answers to a number of questions relating to land use and ownership were provided. One of the basic pieces of information was the amount of woodland in the manor. This was given in a number of different forms which have been studied meticulously by H. C. Darby (1977). For some parts of the country, the area of woodland was given in acres, and for others the length and breadth of woodland was given in leagues, furlongs or perches. In eastern England, woodland was measured by the amount of swine that its acorns and beech-mast could support, while in the South East, it was given as the amount of rent that was payable in return for the right of pannage (pasturage of pigs). In addition to these four widespread methods of assessing woodland, there were also a number of miscellaneous methods.

Following a detailed analysis of the woodland records, Darby concludes that it is impossible to calculate modern acreages from the Domesday figures because the value of the measurements used in Domesday are not known. In order to give some idea of broad woodland distribution, however, he maps the different entries for woodland using conventional signs. More recently, however, Rackham has used the Domesday figures to calculate that England was roughly 15 per cent woodland in 1086. He assumes that a Domesday acre is 1.2 times a modern acre and that the area of woodland given by linear measurements can be calculated by multiplying them, and then multiplying the sum by 0.7 (Rackham 1980, 1986). He agrees with Darby that where the amount of woodland is calculated in relation to swine, it is impossible to give a modern figure. One way around these problems is to compare the amount of woodland given in Domesday with woods whose size is known from other sources such as thirteenth-century records or field evidence. A further complication is that it is the amount of woodland attached to the settlement that is given in the Domesday Book, not the area of individual woods. Moreover, absence of woodland from the survey cannot be taken as absence of woodland on the ground. Because of these difficulties, Domesday evidence is less suited to the study of individual woods than to the distribution of woodland.

Anglo-Saxon Charters

The earliest historical information about woodland is contained in Anglo-Saxon charters, which are the equivalent of modern property deeds. Some date from as early as the seventh century and they continued to be written until around the Conquest in 1066. They are in Latin, Early English or Welsh. Surviving charters have been listed by Sawyer (1968) and regional discussions have been published by Finberg (1961), Hart (1966) and Hooke (1985, 1988). The areas with most charters are the west Midlands and central southern England. There are some charters for South Wales, but few for northern England.

About a third of the surviving charters are provided with boundary clauses. These take the form of perambulations and include references to numerous features such as roads, trees and streams. Hooke (1985) has assessed the number of references to different tree species in the Anglo-Saxon kingdom of the Hwicce in the west Midlands while Rackham (1986a) has mapped landscape features mentioned in all the surviving perambulations and has shown that there are 384 mentions of woodland. The charters are useful in determining the broad distribution of woodland and in a few cases individual surviving ancient woods can be identified.

Scottish Sources

Compared with the situation in England, there is a lack of early documentary sources for the study of Scottish woodland (Millman 1975), but good guides to historical sources are available (Whyte and Whyte 1981, Moody 1986). An extensive bibliography dealing with woodland history was included by Taylor in M. L. Anderson's *A History of Scottish Forestry*. This section outlines a selection of valuable sources peculiar to Scotland and does not include sources which deal with Great Britain as a whole which have already been discussed.

The Scottish Record Office

The national repository for Scottish Records is the Scottish Record Office, HM Register House, Edinburgh EH1 3YY (031 556 6585). It contains Scottish Government records up until 1707, and relevant British Government records for the period after the Act of Union. Until recently there was no system of regional record offices in Scotland and consequently the SRO contains a large amount of local material which in England and Wales would be kept in county record offices. Over 350 collections of private estate papers, for example, are held by the SRO. Many of the records still in private hands have been surveyed by the National Register of Archives (Scotland). Guides to these records, and to the records held at Register House are available at the SRO.

District and Regional Record Offices

Following local government reorganisation in 1975, district and regional authorities have been able to establish archive services but the situation varies from authority to authority. Some regions have done little to organise archive facilities, while others, such as Strathclyde which has established a regional record office at the Strathclyde Regional Archives, Mitchell Library, North St, Glasgow G3 7DN, have brought together central collections.

The Statistical Accounts

The Old Statistical Account covers the period 1791–9 and provides in twenty-one volumes a survey of Scottish parishes, including information on land use. This information was collected by the minister of the Church of Scotland for the parish in response to a list of questions sent out by the editor, Sir John Sinclair. The content and quality of the accounts varies according to the interests of the ministers but they do give valuable information on ancient woodland and tree planting. There is a general index and list of parishes in the last volume (Anderson 1967; Sheail 1980).

The New Statistical Accounts were instigated in the 1830s by the Society for the Sons and Daughters of Clergy. There are fifteen volumes, each of which has its own index and they were published between 1831 and 1845. The area of woodland was given for many parishes and sometimes the area of 'natural' woodland was distinguished from that of plantations. Anderson has tabulated the relevant figures by county and parish and given the results in Appendix C in his *History of Scottish Forestry*.

The Military Survey of Scotland

William Roy was commissioned to make a survey of mainland Scotland between 1747–55 at a scale of about 1in to 1,000yd. This is an important source for the study of Scottish woodland history. Detailed critiques of the map have been made but these have tended to concentrate on the value of the Survey for studying settlement patterns and cultivated land rather than woodland (Whittington and Gibson 1986).

The maps are housed in the British Library in London (copies are held at Edinburgh) and exist in a number of forms:

1 The manuscript map for the area north of the Clyde–Forth line is known as the Protracted Copy. This is difficult to use, because it consists of a number of strips mounted on large rolls of linen.

2 A redrawn and embellished version of the Protracted Copy produced in sheet form.

3 A map of Scotland south of the Clyde–Forth line, produced in sheet form.

4 The Complete Fair Copy, which was brought together between 1829 and 1844 and which was formed by the amalgamation of 2 and 3 above. This copy is in sheet form.

Although the Military Survey is an important source for studying woodland history, it needs to be treated with great care. Walker and Kirby (1987) note that features of relief and land cover, such as woods and plantations, were probably 'sketched in by eye, or copied from existing maps'. Whittington and Gibson (1986) consider that owing to differences between the different copies of the maps, the Protracted and Fair Copy versions should be used in tandem.

Estate Papers

Scottish private estate papers are generally rare for periods before the mid-sixteenth century but are frequent for the later eighteenth and nineteenth centuries. Many types of record such as rentals, accounts, inventories and leases are similar to English and Welsh equivalents. Others such as the records of the Baron and Regality courts, are peculiar to Scotland. Baronies and Regalities were areas of land conferred by royal charters which gave judicial powers to landowners. Whyte and Whyte (1981) point out that 'under a progressive proprietor, baron courts could pass legislation encouraging tenants to undertake improvements such as the planting of trees.' Some of these records are held by the SRO, others are held by private estates.

Estate Maps

Detailed estate maps are not available before the eighteenth century but from about 1750 onwards there was a dramatic increase in the number of maps made and their quality. The SRO holds over 60,000 plans and Adams (1966, 1970, 1974; with Timperley 1988) has produced a descriptive list for this collection. Many other estate maps remain in private hands.

Land Ownership Records

A register of land ownership was set up in the early seventeenth century. This register, which is known as the Register of Sasines, continues in operation and provides a detailed picture of land ownership in Scotland over the past 350 years. Consequently the history of woodland ownership is usually easier to determine in Scotland than in England and Wales. Some property boundaries are described by referring to boundary marks, including trees and shrubs. The register is in two parts: the General Register was kept in Edinburgh, while the Particular Register was kept in specific counties and districts. Indexes to both parts are kept at the SRO. The registers up to 1781 can be consulted freely, later registers can be consulted after the payment of a fee.

Field Surveys

Although much evidence about woodland history can be gathered from the study of maps and records, it is important to combine this information with field evidence. Woods, for example, which have the 'correct' sinuous boundary associated with ancient woodland may in fact be nineteenth-century plantations designed to fit into the landscape according to the prevailing aesthetic theories. More conclusive evidence as to the origin of a wood can be inferred from the characteristics of the vegetation and the nature of historical features such as wood banks.

Field surveys of woodland are needed therefore to assess the historical development of woodland. They are also needed to assess its ecological and conservation value. These factors are interlinked. A survey of a wood's ground flora, for example, is essential for the understanding of woodland ecology but it may also provide evidence of its historical development. This section introduces the main types of woodland survey that can be carried out. For further information on woodland survey K. J. Kirby, *Woodland Survey Handbook*, G. F. Peterken, *Woodland Conservation and Management*, and O. Rackham, *Ancient Woodland: Its History, Vegetation and Uses in England*, should be consulted.

Historical Features: Wood Boundaries

There were strong regional variations in the methods used to make wood boundaries and although the most frequently discussed type is the wood bank, in some parts of the country ancient woods are surrounded by walls, and in others, there seems to be no tradition of making wood boundaries. Where there is a fixed boundary, as in the case of most ancient woods in the south and east, it is much easier to show that a site is ancient than in cases where there is no boundary, as is the case with some of the ancient woods of the uplands.

With compact, lowland woods it is often best, when carrying out a field survey, to start with an assessment of the wood boundary. In the first place, with small woods, this will enable a rapid assessment of the woodland types which are likely to be found in the interior of the wood. Second, it will be possible to assess surrounding land uses, and thirdly, it will be possible to survey the nature of the boundary itself. If any adjoining land is grazed, the wood boundary should be checked to see whether it is stockproof. At the same time, it will be possible to use the characteristics of the wood boundaries as diagnostic features which can, in conjunction with other evidence, help to show whether a wood is ancient.

Wood banks

Many ancient woods are surrounded by ditches and banks. This is especially true of woods in lowland England but such banks are also found in Wales and Scotland. These boundaries are usually combined with a hedge or a fence. Normally, the wood bank would have been made by the owner of the wood as it would be in his interests to keep out grazing animals. Consequently the ditch is found on the outside of the bank and if the wood boundary is also a legal boundary the limit of the wood will normally be the outer edge of the ditch, with the bank itself being part of the wood.

The most extensive study of banks has been made by Rackham (1976, 1980, 1986b) who has shown that the form of the wood bank is often an indication of its age. In general, the more massive the bank the older it is and Rackham considers that many banks were constructed well before 1250. In Wales, the Book of Llandaff, which was compiled in the second half of the twelfth century, includes many references to the edges of woods as land boundaries (Linnard 1982). The range of wood boundaries found in Scotland in the eighteenth and nineteenth centuries is discussed by Anderson (1967).

It is difficult to generalise about banks but they are usually convex in cross-section and are often around 10m (11yd) in width. They rarely exceed 1m (3ft 3in) in height. The exact form of wood banks when first constructed in the medieval period is not known. Over the years erosion will have made them less significant features. Originally the banks would probably have been topped with some sort of live or dead hedge in order to make them stockproof. In most ancient woods, the banks were designed to keep animals out. In deer parks, on the other hand, the banks were built to keep the animals in. Wood banks are relatively easy to find because of their size but it is usually best to follow them in the winter and early spring before the ground vegetation has fully developed. If there are dense brambles, it is often best to wait until after a heavy snow fall has flattened them. The banks are seen very clearly when an area has recently been coppiced.

The coppice on this wood bank at Bradfield Woods, Suffolk, has recently been cut, and the ash tree in the foreground has been cut to form a new pollard tree. The substantial wood bank and ditch has helped to maintain the irregular boundary of the wood over the centuries

Wood banks should be studied in conjunction with old maps of the wood. The sinuous boundaries characteristic of ancient woods often appear from maps to have remained the same for a very long time and such evidence can often be backed up by the field evidence of wood banks. Woods have tended to stay the same shape and size because they were often not owned or occupied by the same people as the surrounding agricultural land. In addition, the massive size of wood banks has itself been a significant factor in conserving the shape of a wood. Indeed in many cases wood banks still exist along the whole length of the boundary of an ancient wood. However, where a section of a wood has been cleared, the new edge often has a less massive wood bank, or no bank at all. Where an ancient wood has grown in size, either by natural succession or planting, the original wood bank may still exist inside the new boundary of the wood.

A study of the layout of wood banks can give an insight into the history of the wood, and show which parts are likely to be oldest. Care must be taken in the interpretation of banks, however, as not all boundaries were on the edge of woods. Large woods were often owned by a number of different people or may be in more than one parish and such ownership and parish boundaries were often marked by wood banks. Wood banks can be treated as archaeological sites and used to trace past activities in an area (Hendry et al 1984). The wide range of wood banks that can be found in quite a small area is shown by Rackham's study of the woods of south east Essex (1986b).

Wood walls

Where stone was readily available, the boundaries of ancient woods were marked by stone walls. Little research has been carried out on the dating of stone walls but where the stone wall follows the sinuous and irregular boundary of an ancient wood exactly it is likely to be of great age. Wood walls are often derelict following years of neglect and all that may remain today is a line of rubble.

In some cases walls were only intended to be temporary. In late eighteenth-century Perthshire, for example, it was a usual practice to enclose newly cut coppice with a stone wall in order to keep out cattle for five or seven years (Anderson 1967). It is difficult to date stone walls, but some research has been carried out on the walls of Roystone Grange, near Ashbourne, Derbyshire (Wildgoose 1987). A study of the sequence of construction of 60km (37 miles)

of limestone walls has enabled a basic classification of five types of wall to be made. When these were mapped, it was possible to reconstruct successive wall patterns from Neolithic times to the present day.

Ridge and furrow

Some ancient woods contain areas where the surface of the ground is corrugated. In the medieval period, and as late as the nineteenth century in some areas, arable land often took the form of a series of ridges and furrows. These were made by the system of ploughing (Mead 1954, Green 1975). Ridge and furrow is important because first, it is an archaeological feature in its own right and secondly, it is a clear indication that the area of woodland concerned is secondary.

First, although research has been carried out into the origin and distribution of ridge and furrow, much work remains to be done. Little is as yet known about regional variations in this feature, or about changes in its form over time. It is therefore necessary to preserve as much of the remaining ridge and furrow as possible. This feature has only survived on sites which have not been recently ploughed. In many parts of the country, ridge or furrow which used to be under old pasture has been destroyed by modern ploughing, and the only remaining ridge and furrow may be within woodland. In several Northamptonshire parishes, for example, ridge and furrow is now only found in woodland (Upex 1984).

Secondly, areas of woodland with ridge and furrow must be secondary (Hooper 1973, Booth 1967). It is therefore a means of distinguishing between areas of ancient woodland which may be primary and those that are secondary and its occurrence should be mapped. It can also help to date when an area became wooded. As a general rule, the wider the ridge, the earlier the feature. If a ridge, measured from the bottom of one furrow to the bottom of the next, is from 10.5m to 12m wide (11½yd to 13yd), it is likely to date from the fifteenth to the seventeenth centuries; if it is as narrow as 2.5m to 3.5m

(2¾yd to 3¾yd) it is likely to date from the nineteenth century (Upex 1984).

Miscellaneous earthworks

A whole range of earthworks can be found in ancient woodland in addition to wood banks and ridge and furrow. Some, such as Iron Age fortifications are, like ridge and furrow, clear indications that the woodland is secondary. Others, such as charcoal hearths, show what the woodland produce was used for in the past (Armstrong 1978, Linnard 1987). In Ecclesall Woods, Sheffield, for example, the presence of nearly eighty whitecoal pits suggests the seventeenth-century use of underwood to make kiln-dried wood for use as fuel in lead-ore hearths (Jones 1986).

Surveys of Flora and Fauna
Species Lists

If accurate lists of species are to be produced for ancient woods, it is essential that they should be surveyed by people who have the ability of identifying a wide range of species within the group of species being surveyed. It may be possible to get help from the local county conservation trust or the regional office of the Nature Conservancy Council. The most complete guide to woodland surveys is K. J. Kirby's *Woodland Survey Handbook*. Many woodland surveys are carried out in a couple of hours and are not as thorough as they might be. If a wood is regularly visited it will be possible to carry out a much fuller assessment of the species growing in it at different times of the year and gradually a complete list of species growing in the wood can be built up (Kirby et al 1986).

It is worth checking with the local conservation trust to see if species lists have already

The walls of ancient woods have been studied less than wood banks. They are difficult to date. This wall is in a wood at Cressbrookdale in Derbyshire. Walls in woods can provide good habitat for insects, small mammals, snails, mosses and lichen, and should not be disturbed.

been made. If so, this survey information can be used as a basis for collecting further information. The records of the local county botanical or historical society should be checked to see if there are any older botanical records for the wood. Many woods have such information from the mid-nineteenth century onwards and this can provide historical evidence for changes in the species found in the wood. If a list of the flowering plants and ferns found in a wood is to be made, it may be helpful to obtain some woodland record cards from the local office of the NCC.

Surveying Different Groups of Species

Most naturalists have an interest in wild flowers and birds and consequently the readily available information on species for many woods relates to these groups. Information on the trees and other vascular plants is particularly important as it forms the basis by which ancient woodland is classified. The less popular groups of species should also, wherever possible, be surveyed. Some, such as the bryophytes (Ratcliffe 1968), lichens (Rose 1976) and snails (Boycott 1934) can include ancient woodland indicators. It is well worth asking an expert in these groups to visit the wood and make a list of the separate species. There are a number of specialist societies which are interested in the various groups of plants and animals: these are listed in the *Directory of British Associations* (1986).

Survey Records

The information collected during field surveys should be recorded and stored carefully. This helps when the time comes to assess whether the management operations carried out have fulfilled the objectives. If, for example, a description of the ground flora of an area of overgrown coppice has been made, it may be possible to see what effects coppicing has on the ground flora by comparing that description with the results of a new survey of the site.

Indicator Species

It has long been recognised that some species are characteristic of ancient woodland. These ancient woodland species are not only of interest in themselves; they can be used, together with documentary evidence, in assessing whether a particular wood is likely to be ancient (Peterken and Game 1984). Indeed, for various parts of the country standard regional lists of ancient woodland indicators are in use.

The use of indicator species in Oxfordshire has been investigated by Gibson (1988). Using a list of indicator species drawn up by the NCC for southern England, he compared the occurrence of such plants in ancient woodland and secondary woodland. The results of this study showed that most individual species were only indicators in the sense that they were more common within ancient woodland than outside. Some ancient woodland indicators, however, were found growing in arable fields and others were never found in ancient woodland.

This study shows that care has to be taken when using indicator species. If there are large populations of indicator species, and the wood appears to be ancient from historical evidence, then the two factors taken together suggest that the wood is ancient. If, on the other hand, the documentary evidence implies that an area of woodland is secondary, the occurrence of a few ancient woodland species cannot be taken as an indication that the wood is really ancient. Indicator species can be an especially important source of information in ancient woods which have been converted to plantations. Here, the woody semi-natural vegetation may have entirely disappeared and the only ecological evidence to back up any historical information that may be available is provided by the ground flora.

Distribution and Form of Trees

Because trees are generally long-lived, they can themselves provide a considerable amount of information about the history of a wood. Areas of native trees and shrubs unevenly scattered in woodland may suggest that it is semi-natural in origin. At the opposite extreme, if a stand consists of only one species and the trees grow in rows, then it is likely to be a plantation. Such evidence should not be taken in isolation as proof that a stand is ancient. Stands composed of trees of semi-natural origin may be shown to be recent by a quick glance at an old map. Stands which are clearly now plantations are often on ancient sites; whether this is so can be discovered by looking at its ground flora and some historical records.

The existence of large old coppice stools can be used as evidence that a wood is ancient. Again, care is needed. Some old stools are in fact the regrowth from standards felled in the early part of the century. Moreover, some areas of coppice were planted in the eighteenth and nineteenth centuries. It is only in conjunction with other ecological and documentary evidence that the existence of old stools can be taken as conclusive evidence that an area is ancient.

Old pollards may be evidence that an area was once managed as wood pasture. If the pollards now occur in dense woodland, then it may be that the wood was once grazed and was much more open. The position of pollards can also be a factor. If they are on the edge of an area of coppice, they should not be taken as evidence that the whole coppice was grazed: many pollards are found on the edge of woods as markers or because they could be browsed from adjoining farmland.

Woodland Classification

In recent years at least four new classifications of woodland have been published (Rackham 1980, Peterken 1981, Bunce 1982, NVC 1988). The classification in widest use at present is probably Peterken's, which enables semi-natural ancient woodland to be divided into one of twelve groups, based on the composition of the semi-natural coppice and pollards present in the stand. Full details of this classification are set out by Peterken (1981) and Kirby (1988).

A more general classification is provided by the woodland section of the National Vegetation Classification (Rodwell, in press). Unlike the Peterken classification, this is based on an assessment of all the vascular plants, bryophytes and larger lichens present in a stand, rather than just the trees and shrubs. This means that the classifier has to be able to identify a much larger range of species than is necessary for the Peterken classification. Because of this broader base, however, the NVC is applicable to all types of ancient woodland: plantations are seen as modifications of the basic twenty woodland communities. A simplified key to the NVC is available. Further details of woodland classification are given in the books that accompany this volume (Marren 1990, 1991).

Pollen Analysis

The scientific analysis of pollen preserved in peat and soils has been a crucial factor in the development of our understanding of vegetational change in the post-glacial period and earlier (Godwin 1975). Until recently, pollen analysis has been used for the study of vegetation change at the regional rather than the local level. Techniques have now been developed, however, which enable studies of historical vegetation change to be made for particular woods (Bradshaw 1988, Hannon and Bradshaw 1989, Moseley and Moore 1988).

These methods make use of pollen collected from within woods. They rely on the fact that under woodland conditions pollen only travels 20–30m (22–33yd) from its source. The sorts of site which are suitable for this type of analysis fall into three main categories: 1 Small, wet hollows; 2 accumulations of acidic humus and 3 soils of low biological activity. This new form of pollen analysis can provide striking details about vegetation history.

Part III
MANAGING ANCIENT WOODLAND

4 Nature Conservation and Ancient Woodland

This chapter introduces some of the basic considerations that need to be taken into account when managing ancient woodland in the interests of nature conservation. The first two sections outline the value of management for nature conservation and the role of non-intervention reserves. These are followed by an assessment of the impact of natural factors such as fire and disease. The chapter goes on to discuss the relative value for nature conservation of native and non-native trees and natural regeneration and planting. Further sections include the nature conservation value of dead wood; site factors, such as the location and size of a wood; the design of management plans for ancient woodland and the use of herbicides.

Management for Conservation
Management or Non-intervention?
It is often thought that people interested in nature conservation wish to prevent the management of woodland and to turn all woods into untouched reserves. This is almost the opposite of the truth. Management often brings direct benefits to wildlife and it is these benefits that allow a compromise to be reached between conservation and timber growing (Steele and Peterken 1982). There is some value in having non-intervention areas and a number of species do benefit from neglect (Sterling and Hambler 1988), but managed woods usually contain a richer variety of habitats within a limited area and thus more species than unmanaged woods.

In neglected woods the rides become shaded; light-demanding herbs and shrubs are lost from the stands and the species associated with open spaces and early stages in the succession to woodland are much reduced (Warren 1985). Furthermore, in some woods neglect has allowed certain undesirable species, such as rhododendron, to spread.

The management history of any wood is a crucial factor in determining whether a wood is important for nature conservation. The tradition of wood pasture management, for example, provided the conditions in which the large trees characteristic of original woodland could survive and with them the great trunks, rotting cores, dead branches and other habitats which they provide. As a result, the old parklands and unenclosed forest woods are the main refuges for the fauna of mature timber.

Coppice management was complementary to wood pasture. In coppices there were relatively few very old trees, except perhaps for a few pollards around the wood boundary. On the other hand, the shrubs, trees and ground flora were relatively unaffected by grazing. Thus coppice woods tend to retain their original ground flora but have an impoverished dead-wood fauna.

Woodland clearance and management has over the years led to the decline in a large number of species of insects and mammals and to low levels of lichens and certain trees such as lime. Management has not only influenced the survival of the original woodland flora and fauna but has, in some cases, enriched it. Indeed some ancient woods are probably richer as wildlife habitats than the natural woods from which they descended. This has come about for two reasons. First, any management, but especially coppicing, creates open spaces in woods at a faster rate than would happen in natural woods. This means that there are more clearings and consequently more young growth in managed woods and these are both especially rich phases in the sequence of stand growth.

Second, woodland management has resulted in the creation of rides in order to gain access to the woodland. These form an entirely artificial type of habitat made up of grassland and tall herb vegetation. In ancient woods they have often had two hundred years or more in which to develop into rich habitats by means of grassland species colonising from neighbouring pastures and meadows.

This general support for management rather than neglect should not be be taken as support for all kinds of management. Many forestry and agricultural operations are very damaging to ancient woodland. These include the planting of trees and shrubs not native to the area or of foreign provenance; the clearance and killing of old coppice stools and the removal of all mature trees and dead wood. None of these types of management are approved of in ancient woodland from a conservation point of view.

Continuity of management

Habitat continuity is an important consideration for nature conservation. To take a simple example, it may be that all the plants of herb paris in a wood die as a result of the heavy shading by a planted stand of pure conifers. What will happen if, decades later, the conifers are replaced by native broadleaves and the ground once again becomes suitable for the growth of herb paris? If, as is often the case, the wood is surrounded by agricultural land, and there is no suitable adjoining habitat for the herb paris, then it is likely that the plant will not return because it has no effective means of colonising from other more distant woods. In other words, herb paris, as with many woodland plants and invertebrates which exist as a scatter of isolated populations, can be permanently extinguished by temporary periods of unsympathetic man-

agement. With some plant species, of course, viable seed may remain buried in the soil for many years until suitable conditions return for their germination. This is not true, however, for invertebrates which have no 'buried seed' equivalent and therefore need to be kept permanently on the site.

Many species are able to move from wood to wood because, in the case of plants, they have efficient seed dispersal mechanisms and in the case of animals, they are able to move relatively long distances. Continuity of habitat is not necessarily important for the long-term survival of these species on particular woodland sites. If we consider good colonists such as wood avens or blackbirds, for example, they may or may not be evicted from a site by a rotation of conifers, but, if they were, they would return rapidly when suitable conditions were restored.

Conservation of Groups of Species and Rare Species

Some woods contain extremely rare plants and animals, and in these cases the woodland management should take account of their needs so that they can survive and even increase in number. The larvae of the purple emperor butterfly, for example, feed on goat willow and the adults feed on the leaf secretions of oak. Willmott (1987) considers that to conserve the species, which has declined rapidly in recent years, the best policy is to have patches of mature goat willow as well as mature oak in ancient woodland.

Other woods are renowned for a particular group of species. Many lowland ancient woods are famous for their spring flowers and often the main aim of woodland management is to conserve and improve the ground flora by manipulating the different levels of the tree canopy. In other cases it is butterflies or the dead-wood invertebrates that are the important groups. Often the best way to encourage these particular species or groups of species is to continue to manage ancient woodland along traditional lines or to reintroduce such management.

Non-intervention
Value of Non-intervention Reserves

The character of the natural woodland is known to have changed dramatically as the climate fluctuated and additional tree species arrived (Godwin 1975). As well as such long-term changes, there are the natural processes of regeneration and decay, including the recovery of woodland from gale damage, which take place in the medium term over a few hundred years.

Non-intervention reserves are essential for the study of these ecological processes because they are the only woods where such natural processes are not obscured by human activity (Peterken and Backmeroff 1988). Non-intervention areas also benefit those species characteristic of 'mature' high forest.

Very few reserves have been set up with non-intervention as their main aim, though there are many woods which have remained largely unmanaged for well over fifty years. Where such reserves have been set up, the long-term aim is to allow the woodland to develop with as little human interference as possible. Ideally the sites chosen for this purpose should be:

1   large enough to exclude or reduce outside influences;
2   already in a fairly natural state in terms of structure or composition;
3   owned by an organisation which can justify and support this objective for a very long time. In practice it is very difficult to ensure such ownership.

A good example of non-intervention management is provided by Lady Park Wood near the Forest of Dean in Gloucestershire (Peterken and Jones 1987). Other examples are some of the unenclosed New Forest woods (Putman 1986, Tubbs 1987) and parts of the Black Wood of Rannoch (Peterken and Stace 1987), although in these cases grazing has an important influence on woodland development and in this respect they are not strictly non-intervention areas. Steele and Peterken (1982) suggest that only 3 per cent of the total area of broadleaved woodland need be non-intervention woodland. This small proportion belies the conservation value of these non-intervention areas.

Unmanaged Woods Outside Special Reserves

Many ancient woods, of course, are not reserves and yet are gaining natural characteristics through neglect. Some of these are undoubtedly written off by their owners as not worth managing in a commercial sense, while for others management is in abeyance until circumstances change, or sufficient information is available to make management decisions.

In addition, there are many areas of woodland which are part of commercially managed blocks but for various reasons are left untouched. Although not specifically chosen as non-intervention reserves, these areas can be of scientific value, especially if detailed records are kept of their development. Lack of management may, in some cases, be gradually reducing the conservation value of these woods but this gradual deterioration is much better than the considerable loss of valuable habitat there would be if these areas were, for example, replanted with conifers. If left

Lady Park Wood, in the Wye Valley, Gloucestershire, is a National Nature Reserve. This wood was set aside by the Forestry Commission as an area to receive no management in 1944. The top photograph is a view of the wood from the other side of the river. It shows how the wood is growing on the steep cliffs adjoining the River Wye. The photograph below shows one of the flatter parts of the interior of the wood. All dead wood is left to rot on the ground. The main trees found in the wood include ash, lime, beech, sycamore, oak, elm, maple and birch. Woodland surveys have been carried out at various dates. Comparison of the results shows that stand development over the past 45 years has been affected by a series of factors including disease, unstable trees falling down the steep slopes and windblow (Peterken and Jones 1987 and 1989)

unmanaged, it will at least be possible, at some future date, to salvage the conservation interest of the wood.

Non-intervention Areas Within Woods

In the past it was common for an entire wood to be intensively managed. Trees would be regularly coppiced or pollarded at relatively short intervals; the ground vegetation would be grazed; the dead wood and small twigs would be collected for firewood and the animals would be hunted. Not all these practices are desirable from a conservation point of view. Moreover, because of the difficulty in finding sufficient labour and the low value of much woodland produce, it is often costly to bring the whole of a wood back under management. To overcome this problem to the advantage of conservation certain parts of a wood may be set aside as non-intervention areas.

Sometimes it is quite easy to choose which part of a wood should remain unmanaged. It is ecologically better to have such stands within a wood than on its edge. Non-ecological factors may also be important. Thus those parts of a wood that are difficult to manage because of location (inaccessible stands cut off from the rest of the property by a motorway, railway or river) or site (stands on very steep slopes or very wet ground) may be ideal as non-intervention zones. This will not, however, always be the case. The steep, wet or inaccessible stands may be formed of semi-natural vegetation which it is necessary to manage in order to conserve. Difficulty of management should not be the only reason for leaving an area unmanaged.

Public Access and Non-intervention

In very strict terms it could be argued that people should not be allowed to visit areas kept as non-intervention reserves. There is a possibility that they will steal dead wood, damage natural vegetation, bring in seeds from outside and generally cause difficulties to woodland managers. In practice, areas of unmanaged woodland often develop an attractive atmosphere of wilderness and it is difficult to keep people out.

A general compromise might be to ensure that as far as possible visitors keep to designated paths. Unmanaged woodland will eventually be full of old and dead trees which will be potentially dangerous. It is sensible to make sure that no public rights of way pass through such stands and to be aware of the owner's legal liability in respect of any damage caused by falling trees (Griffin and Watkins 1986).

Natural Factors

Very few strictly 'natural' changes can take place in British ancient woodland. Even if an area is left unmanaged, the lack of management is the result of a series of human decisions. It is possible, however, to distinguish between those changes that are the intentional or unintentional result of management actions, and those that are not. The second category includes changes caused by such factors as climate and weather; fire; pollution; disease; grazing by undomesticated animals; the life cycles of trees, plants and animals and so forth.

These natural factors can affect both managed and unmanaged woods. In managed woods natural factors may cause changes that the manager requires or they may disrupt or destroy the fruits of much labour. In unmanaged woods they are the main cause of woodland change.

Fire

In prehistoric times, fire was probably often used to destroy natural woodland and convert it to other land uses. Today, it is much less important. Woodland fires are seasonal in occurrence and are most likely to take place in February, March or April (Parsons and Evans 1977). This is perhaps surprising but by spring the dead vegetation, which has accumulated in the autumn and winter, will have become dried by the frosts and strong winds of March and April.

In general, apart from during periods of drought, ancient broadleaved woodland is not very combustible and large-scale woodland change is unlikely to result from fire. However, ancient woods on acid soils, with a field layer of bracken or bilberry, are more combustible than those on clay soils and fire can be an important management consideration in ancient pine woods.

Disease

The most dramatic change caused by disease in recent years has been the death of many elm trees in Great Britain through Dutch elm disease (Burdekin 1983, Brasier and Webber 1987). Although many of the elms are now showing signs of regrowth, the disease has had an important impact on the ecology of much ancient woodland (Rackham 1989).

The effects of most other diseases are much less noticeable as disease is a normal element of natural woodland. *Armillaria*, which is commonly known as the honey fungus, for example, has been an important means of bringing about the decay of dead wood in semi-natural woodland for thousands of years. Other diseases are of more recent origin in Great Britain, and may be a cause of change in the way a woodland develops. Rackham (1980) suggests that the oak mildew fungus, which was introduced in 1908, may be one of the reasons for the lack of successful regeneration of oak seedlings within many ancient woods.

Climate and Weather

There have been massive long-term changes in the species making up the natural woodland cover since the retreat of the ice and these are closely related to the changing climate of Britain over that period. For at least the last six thousand years, however, human activity has been more important than climate as a factor determining woodland change.

Variations in the weather are still of critical importance in terms of woodland ecology. The length of the growing season depends on temperature, rainfall and light. Moreover,

These ash trees at Wyndcliff in Gwent blew down in a gale of 1984. Much more extensive damage was caused in the famous storms of February 1976 and October 1987. In natural woodland, such events would be one of the main causes of woodland change

extremes of weather are a potent influence on woodland change. Strong winds such as those of February 1976 or October 1987 can fell substantial areas of woodland. Heavy snow can cause the collapse of overgrown coppice or pollards; drought can kill young trees, especially if they have been recently planted; and small areas of ground can be kept free of trees because they are frost hollows.

In management terms weather has an influence on the timing of operations. It can be especially important, for example, in a clay area when deciding at what time of year timber can be removed from a wood. More generally bad weather reduces the speed at which coppice and timber can be harvested.

Grazing

Grazing can have a very significant effect on the ecology of ancient woodlands (Pigott 1983, Putnam 1986). Where heavy grazing is allowed there will probably be a lack of natural regeneration of trees and shrubs even though other conditions such as seed supply, soil and light are suitable. Selective grazing

Rhododendron ponticum L. is the most prolific introduced evergreen shrub. It thrives in woodland conditions, and in many parts of Britain it can completely dominate the shrub layer of whole woods. It is thought to have been introduced in 1763. W. J. Bean, in his standard work Trees and shrubs hardy in the British Isles *(1951) pointed out that 'in spite of its great beauty the Pontic rhododendron needs occasionally the curb of a strong hand'. More recently, the shrub has become recognised as a major threat to the conservation value of many woods. This picture shows an area of oak woodland at Maintwrog, Gwynedd. Dense rhododendron can be seen in the background, while the foreground has been cleared*

tends to reduce the number of species growing in the field layer. It can also bring about changes in the relative proportions of tree species (Rackham 1975, Peterken and Jones 1989) (see Chapter 5). Grazing is discussed more fully in Chapter 8.

Changes in Tree Species Composition

Over the years the proportion of trees of different species will tend to vary as individual trees die and regeneration takes place. Although the study of natural succession has long been one of the cornerstones of ecology, little is known about these changes in species composition in British woods (Watt 1923, Tansley 1939).

Some trees, such as birch, are known to spread into new areas by taking advantage of the light conditions and soil disturbance associated with gaps caused by windblow. Similar changes in species composition can take place in managed woodland through natural regeneration. This happened on a large scale

in areas of ancient woodland felled in the war. Birch spread into the felled areas and, in many neglected ancient woods, this wartime generation of birch is now beginning to die. In some of these woods there is little chance of the birch regenerating unless some felling of the surrounding overgrown coppice takes place or there is extensive wind damage.

Other trees, such as the English elm and aspen, spread by the growth of suckers from the roots. English elm was much planted in hedgerows, and has invaded many ancient woods through the growth of suckers. Such invasion has been halted in most areas by the spread of Dutch elm disease. Aspen grows vigorously from root suckers and is quickly able to take advantage of relatively small gaps in the tree canopy (Koop 1987).

Native and Non-native Trees
Conservation Value

Trees are described as native if they arrived in Britain without the assistance of humans. Many common trees, including most conifers, are not native. Some of these non-native trees, and especially sycamore, spread into ancient woodland by natural regeneration. Most, however, were introduced by planting. In terms of nature conservation there are a number of reasons for, as far as possible, excluding non-native trees from ancient woodland. Non-native trees take up space which could be used by native trees. They can have adverse effects on the semi-natural ground flora and the associated invertebrates. Planted conifers often have a particularly detrimental effect because they tend to cast a much heavier shade than native species other than beech and hornbeam. In general terms, therefore, ancient woodland should be managed with the long-term aim of eliminating non-native species.

Treatment of Non-native Trees and Shrubs in Ancient Woods

The treatment of non-native trees and shrubs needs to vary according to the effect that they have on the ecology and conservation value of the ancient woodland concerned. Where conifers have been planted, the general aim should be to remove them as soon as is feasible (see Chapter 7). Many introduced trees do not regenerate naturally and so do not pose a management problem once they have been felled. It is possible, for example, to retain the occasional specimen sequoia, Norway spruce or tulip tree as regeneration from these trees is unlikely to cause a management problem.

The situation is very different with *Rhododendron ponticum* which is extremely damaging to woodland. In many parts of Britain it grows and regenerates profusely, and can completely take over the shrub layer of whole woods (Shaw 1984). Little will grow under it and, wherever possible, it should be removed although this can be an expensive and difficult process.

The case of sycamore is less clear cut: it has now been well established in Britain for at least five hundred years and, if it is not allowed to dominate a woodland, appears to do little harm to the ground flora (Taylor 1985). The main problem with sycamore is that it takes up space which could be used by native trees. It also offends many people's sense of historical aesthetics. In some woods it is one of the few indications that the species present are not 'unchanged' from the early medieval period.

The question is, should ancient woodland be conserved in a state which approximates to its pre-sycamore state, in which case the sycamore should be weeded out, or should the spread of sycamore into a wood by natural regeneration be seen as one of the many 'natural' changes taking place in the woodland? The treatment of sycamore regeneration is discussed in Chapter 6.

Non-native Trees Outside Ancient Woods

Some recent woodland is semi-natural and can be of great nature conservation interest. Non-native trees should not be planted in such areas. There is little reason, however, to exclude non-native trees from plantations

GLASGOW

on recent woodland sites. Indeed, to do so would, in many cases, be futile as many have always consisted of non-native trees.

Where recent woodland adjoins an ancient woodland, there may be a danger that non-native trees such as sycamore or Turkey oak will naturally spread across the boundary. Uprooting such regeneration is very time-consuming and, in nature conservation terms, it is not advisable to plant non-native trees which freely regenerate near to ancient woods.

Non-local Trees

The management of ancient woodland should aim to conserve the variation in the existing semi-natural woodland types. In many ancient woods certain tree species will tend to grow on particular types of soil. It is not good conservation practice to plant or encourage the regeneration of trees on soil types on which they do not normally occur. Similarly, on a larger scale, some species, such as Scots pine and bird cherry are natu-

This shows part of Sherwood Forest, near Edwinstowe, Nottinghamshire, which has been replanted with oak in the form of a map of Great Britain. The young oak trees, which have been grown from local acorns, have been planted in tree shelters to speed up their establishment. In the background can be seen a number of the ancient Sherwood oaks, some of which are dead.

rally distributed in Scotland and northern England, while others, such as hornbeam and beech, are naturally found in the south. Trees with such regional distributions should not be planted or encouraged to regenerate in ancient woods outside their natural range.

Natural Regeneration and Planting

The preferred method of restocking for nature conservation is natural regeneration because it helps maintain the continuity of both species and genetic stock. Unfortunately, it can be an uncertain method of restocking and this has to be taken into account when making commercial decisions about its use.

Where natural regeneration is successful it is cheaper than planting: transplants do not have to be bought; labour is not needed for planting; weeding costs can be reduced. The use of natural regeneration usually entails fairly small-scale working and where group felling systems are used, the groups are often between a tenth and half a hectare (¼–1¼ acres) in size. This is beneficial in conservation terms but can mean increased costs because of loss of economies of scale.

By far the most frequently used method of restocking an area of woodland is the planting of transplants. This is second best to natural regeneration from the point of view of conservation but is usually a very much more economic and certain method of restocking. It is, moreover, a method all foresters are accustomed to using.

When an ancient semi-natural wood is felled and converted to a plantation some of its most valuable features are damaged or destroyed. The most obvious loss is the mixture of native tree and shrub species. There is also a loss of mature timber and dead-wood habitat as large old trees and massive coppice stools are generally removed. It is impossible to predict the long-term effects of converting a whole semi-natural wood into a plantation because in most cases the conversion has been too recent. However, it is known that while many species will thrive, the true woodland species such as shade-bearing plants, timber-using fauna and native tree and shrub species are likely to suffer. As a general rule, planting should be restricted to those parts of ancient woods where planting has taken place previously. It should not be carried out in areas of semi-natural woodland where there is no evidence of past planting.

If it is desired to change to more valuable species or grow species of known good provenances, it is possible to carry out limited 'enrichment', ie, planting of trees within a matrix of natural regeneration. Preferably such enrichment should not be carried out in ancient semi-natural woodland but it can be beneficial where woodland has been heavily modified by planting or selective storing in the past (see Chapter 5). Some of the beechwoods in the Chilterns, for example, could well benefit from the planting of other species such as field maple or gean which are native to the area, but which are unlikely to regenerate naturally (Hornby 1987).

Genetic factors

One aim of nature conservation is to retain natural genetic variety. For this reason it is always preferable to restock stands with species of local provenance, especially in semi-natural woodland. The problem is that many stands contain trees which were planted and which might not be of local origin. The safest course is to restock stands by natural regeneration or to use plants grown from seed collected on the site. In the case of oak there is some evidence that trees of good form, from a silvicultural point of view, are likely to have been planted and some acorns should therefore be collected from trees of poor form. Seed should also be collected from old coppice or pollards.

Dead Wood and Over-mature Trees
Conservation Value

In natural woodland the trees grow old and decay, consequently a large range of species associated with rotting trees, whether standing or fallen, has evolved. Over-mature trees provide homes for hole-nesting birds and bats as well as being a food source for numerous insects and fungi. Rotting logs can also be good sites for the establishment of seedling trees.

Amounts of Dead Wood in Different Types of Woodland

In woodland managed for timber, dead-wood habitat is usually very poorly represented. In coppice stands, for example, most of the stems will be under fifty years old, while even the standards will be less than one hundred and fifty years old, which is less than half of the natural lifespan of trees such as the oak.

It is very important to maintain supplies of dead timber in ancient woodland. A large range of species are associated with dead and dying timber. Whole tree trunks are especially important because they allow for continuity of habitat. This photograph shows one of the large old dead oaks of Sherwood Forest, with a fallen trunk amongst the bracken in the foreground.

Where woodland nature reserves are managed as non-intervention areas the amount of dead wood and old trees will gradually increase. For the majority of sites, however, this is unlikely to be a satisfactory management technique but there is usually scope for increasing the amount of dead wood and over-mature trees.

As continuity of habitat is so important for many species which use dead wood, large blocks of timber, such as whole tree trunks, are more useful than lots of small pieces. Consequently, it is more important to maintain the supply of dead wood in a mature high forest or wood pasture than to create new supplies of dead wood in a coppice where there has not been much dead wood in the past. Nevertheless, because of the general lack of dead wood in coppices in the past, the dead wood that exists today in the form of old coppice stools and over-mature standards should be maintained.

Increasing the Amount of Dead Wood
The easiest and quickest way to increase the amount of dead-wood habitat is to leave a proportion of poor quality cut timber and poles to rot on the site. The best procedure to follow depends on the size of the poles and timber concerned. The larger logs and stumps should simply be left to rot on the ground. Smaller branches and lop and top can be piled up. This gives a greater con-

centration of dead wood at a particular site and may provide shelter for nesting birds and small mammals. The piles should be carefully sited: if a pile is put in the wrong place it can be inconvenient for a number of years. Other possible disadvantages are that the ground flora under the pile of wood may be destroyed, and the piles make ideal cover for rabbits (see Chapter 5).

In general, the dead wood should be left to decay in partial shade. Standing dead trees or logs left in the open can dry out and provide relatively poor habitat for invertebrates. Dead standing trees can be created by removing a ring of bark from the bole of a tree. In some instances, such as when a wood contains a large sycamore of poor timber quality, ring-barking can get rid of the unwanted tree and provide useful dead-wood habitat. Another possibility is to start making some pollards, which can then be cut at frequent intervals (see Chapter 8). These need not take up much space and the pollarding will help to maintain the bole for a long period during which time there is a chance for wood-using insects and lichens to colonise. Another way of obtaining dead wood is to allow small areas of quick-growing trees such as birch and goat willow to regenerate and grow. These trees, and the birch in particular, are short-lived and provide dead wood relatively quickly.

Dead Wood and Danger
In broadleaved woodland, the species which consume dead wood tend to be different from those which attack living trees, so leaving dead wood does not necessarily pose a threat to surrounding commercial woodland. In some cases, it may not be possible to leave trees with large dead overhanging branches or rotten trunks, even though this might be in the best conservation interests, because of the threat to public safety. Where pruning or felling of these trees is unavoidable, the cut branches should be left, if possible, in the shade close to the butt of the tree so that there is the best chance for the recolonisation of other branches of the tree as they become

suitable for dead-wood insects. Cut trunks should similarly be left lying. Sometimes it will be possible for a large tree to be safely pollarded rather than felled completely, so that at least the bole or trunk is retained.

Site Factors
Location
However rich an ancient wood may be in terms of numbers of species, or historical records, it may be very difficult to manage properly because of its location. An extreme case would be a wood which had no access because it was on the triangle of ground at the junction of two railways or motorways. In these instances, there would be an overriding case for having a non-intervention management policy. Much more likely are the cases where there is no suitable access to a wood. Removal of timber may require complicated negotiations with surrounding landowners. Other woods may have too much access. Woods in the depths of the country may have many rights of way and be overused by horse riders. If they are located on the fringe of towns, they may have problems of vandalism, motor-bike racing; fire; rubbish and so forth. These can cause considerable management problems. If possible, however, such sites should be managed as a way of publicising the conservation of woodland. There are a number of books which deal with the special problems of managing woodland in suburbs and towns (Irving 1985, Countryside Commission 1981, Emery 1986).

Intensive use by the public can cause damage to ancient woodlands but other consequences of a wood's location may be even more severe. A wood near a small market town could be threatened by the construction of a by-pass; woods adjoining limestone quarries may be affected by limestone dust; woods in certain parts of the country could be destroyed for open-cast coal-mining. In none of these cases would even freehold ownership by a conservation organisation ensure that the piece of ancient woodland was conserved. The location of a wood can also have a positive effect on its conservation value. If a wood is surrounded by unimproved grassland, for example, it is likely to have a higher conservation value than if it were surrounded by intensively farmed arable land.

Soils

The type of soil on which woodland is found is a critical factor influencing woodland type, and the flora and fauna found in the wood. Unfortunately, however, the soils of ancient woodland have received remarkably little attention (Ball and Stevens 1981). Soil maps of the whole of Britain are available at the 1:250,000 scale, but coverage at the scales of 1:50,000 and 1:25,000 is rather patchy. For England and Wales, maps and monographs are available from the Soil Survey and Land Research Centre, Cranfield Rural Institute, Silsoe, Bedford MK45 4DT (0525 60428). For Scotland, the equivalent information is available from the Macaulay Land Use Research Institute, Craigiebuckler, Aberdeen AB9 2QJ (0224 318611).

The soils of ancient woodland, especially primary woodland, are important for soil scientists because they are relatively undisturbed. They have, of course, been influenced by humans through such factors as grazing, fire and woodland management, but they have not been subject to the frequent ploughing associated with arable and intensive pasture agriculture.

Ball and Stevens (1981) suggest that the uses of ancient woodland soils to soil scientists can be put into four main groups. They are useful:

1 as benchmark soils for the comparative study of soil development;
2 as archive soils which preserve sources of historic information (Bradshaw 1988, Hendry et al 1984, Limbrey 1978);
3 as monitor soils for the study of the present situation and future change;
4 as display soils for educational use.

The type of soil will affect management of ancient woodland. On some soils, such

as those associated with alder flushes, care must be taken to ensure that damage is not caused by management operations such as coppicing and timber extraction. With clay soils the sheer difficulty of moving materials along rides, and danger of damaging ride vegetation, is likely to restrict the extraction of poles and timber to periods when the soils have dried.

Size

There has been much discussion about the optimum size of woodland nature reserves (Helliwell 1976). Most of this is irrelevant in the case of a particular ancient wood because the size of the wood has been determined by historical factors which cannot be changed. In general terms, in comparing the quality of different ancient woods, the larger the block of ancient woodland, the better the potential conservation value.

Larger woods are likely to have a greater total number of species; larger populations of individual species; more diversity of habitat; and be less affected by adjoining land uses than small woods. Even so, some small ancient woods are of much greater conservation value than some large ones. Size is also, of course, an important consideration in the management of a wood. It is a crucial factor when determining the amount of labour that is needed, the layout of felling coupes, the position of extraction routes and the amount of woodland produce.

Shape

In Chapters 2 and 3 it was shown that a wood's shape can be an important clue when working out its history. As with size the shape of an ancient wood is something that has to be accepted. In nature conservation terms, the most important attribute of shape is probably the length of the edge of the wood in relation to the total area.

Long wood boundaries have advantages and disadvantages. The main advantage is that the longer the edge of the wood, the greater the amount of edge habitat and this can be very important for some bird and insect species. The disadvantage of long woodland edges is that they are relatively expensive to manage, and they mean that a greater proportion of the wood can be prone to damage from spray drift and other agricultural operations (see Chapter 9).

Management Plans

Many ancient woods, especially if they are nature reserves or SSSIs, already have some sort of nature conservation management plan, but most do not. It is certainly worthwhile making such a plan as they help to clarify the manager's aims and objectives for the woodland; enable relatively small management decisions to be put in a broader framework and act as a reminder of what work has been carried out for both current and future managers. It may be thought that a plan would be a waste of time for a small wood which the manager knows well. However, it is easy for even quite straightforward management

operations and aims to be forgotten over a couple of years. This is especially true when there is a change in woodland manager; the benefits of such plans for future managers must be considered. This section outlines the basic principles behind management plans. A more detailed introduction to site management plans for nature conservation is available from the Nature Conservancy Council (Reed 1988).

A management plan should consist of three main sections. The first of these is a simple list of general information; the second is an assessment of its conservation status. This should include a site description, an evaluation of the wood and an outline of the manage-

Many areas of ancient woodland have wet soils, as is the case with this overgrown alder coppice in Methven Wood, near Perth. Care must be taken to ensure that damage is not caused by management operations such as coppicing and timber extraction

ment objectives. The third section consists of the prescription, in other words, the operations that need to be carried out to fulfil the management objectives. Management plans can be very detailed and complicated, as may be the case of nature reserves of national importance, or they can be relatively simple, as might be the case with a small privately owned ancient woodland.

General Information

Most woodland managers already have a considerable amount of information about their wood. Although this cache of information could be seen as the first part of the management plan, it is probably better to abstract the most significant information and use this brief edited description as the first part. The information should include a description of the location of the wood, the numbers of relevant Ordnance Survey map sheets, nature conservation status, area, ownership and tenure, access and rights of way and name of manager. The bringing together of this sort of information not only makes it easier to consult but also shows up any gaps in knowledge that can be filled at a later date.

Conservation Status

The second section of the plan should include a brief description of the wood and list the presence of any species of particular importance for nature conservation. It can include a brief summary of any historical information and the results of any ecological surveys. It should also list the management objectives for the wood and the general way in which these objectives are to be met. The objectives depend on the interests of the owner. Nature conservation objectives might include, for instance, the maintenance and improvement of the ground flora or the protection of a particularly rare invertebrate. Often these objectives will be combined with others such as the maintenance of an historic landscape or the production of high quality timber.

The management options used to fulfil these objectives will vary according to the type of woodland and the interests of the owner. If an objective was the maintenance and improvement of the ground flora, for example, the management option could include the resumption of coppicing in a derelict coppice or the removal of conifers from a replanted wood.

Prescription

The third part of the management plan should be a list of the specific operations needed to fulfil the objectives and management options set out in the second section. If, for example, one of the management options was the reintroduction of coppicing in a compartment of the wood, then this third section would detail the number of stages in which this coppicing was to take place; the time of year; the labour to be used and, possibly, the markets for the coppice poles. Similarly, for ride management, this section of the plan would state specifically which parts of the rides were to be mown and at what time of the year.

Maps

Maps are a most important part of any management plan because they are an efficient means of storing and displaying information. For the descriptive section of the plan, they can be used to show the ownership boundaries; access points; site factors; woodland type; rides and so forth. Maps can also be used to show which parts of the wood are of high conservation value, which are to be left as non-intervention areas, which are to be coppiced and which are to be converted to high forest. Maps should also be used to show where specific management is to take place and where it has happened in the past. Maps of proposed work are necessary when applying to the Forestry Commission for permission to fell or for grant aid.

The best scale of map to use for marking basic site details is usually the OS 1:10,000 series. For areas where this is still not available it is usually possible to buy the similar

1:10,650 maps. Maps of these scales may be used to indicate ownership and stand boundaries, water courses and the positions of rides. For more detailed mapping work, the best scale is the OS 1:2,500 series. This is available for much of the country, but not the upland moors. It is especially useful because it shows the area of separate parcels of land in hectares and acres (see Chapter 2 for further information about these map series).

Flexibility

The study of woodland ecology is constantly developing. Knowledge of the habitat requirements of rare species may require changes in the management plan. In addition unforeseen natural changes such as the gale damage which devastated many woods in south-east England in October 1987 take place and these may make sections of management plans obsolete. Plans should therefore be sufficiently flexible to allow for changes in policies and operations and the management needed to fulfil them. They should usually cover a five-year period.

The Use of Herbicides in Ancient Woodland

Herbicides are used by conservation organisations such as the NCC within ancient woodland (Cooke 1986). They are also frequently used by foresters (Sale, Tabbush and Lane 1986). Although the use of herbicides is always potentially harmful to the nature conservation interest of an ancient wood, they can be a useful management tool. A list of herbicides, which are dealt with by Cooke (1986), and can be used in ancient woodland is given in the Appendix on p145.

The use of herbicides for conservation involves a different philosophy to their use in commercial forestry. In conservation, the herbicide is generally used to kill particular individual species: the bulk of the surrounding vegetation should not be affected. In commercial forestry the opposite is the case: the herbicide is used to promote the growth of individual young trees by killing the bulk

of the vegetation that is likely to compete with them.

Herbicides can be used in ancient woods for:

1 the control of invasive species such as sycamore and rhododendron;
2 the spot treatment with spray or granules of the area immediately around the base of transplants, but only if the tree spacing is more than 3m (3¼yd). If such spot treatments are used where there is denser planting, too great an area of the ground flora is killed.

One of the main problems with using herbicides is uncertainty; it may be difficult to predict with accuracy the effect on either the target plants or the surrounding vegetation (Watt, Kirby and Savill 1988). No herbicide is specific to a single species: all affect other species to some extent. In addition, the effects of the herbicide depend not only on its inherent toxicity but also on how dilute it is when applied; what the weather conditions are like; the season of the year; and how it is actually applied to the plant. Some small trial applications of the herbicide may be necessary and if these are successful it will then be possible to proceed on a larger scale. Such trials should only be undertaken within the constraints of the label instructions.

Toxicity to Humans and Animals

The appropriate and specified protective clothing should be worn when using any herbicide and care must be taken to avoid contact with the skin. Users should always wash immediately after using the herbicide. Most herbicides, when applied according to the manufacturers' instructions, have a low toxicity to animals. No herbicide has the combination of persistence, toxicity and tendency to bio-accumulate, which made insecticides such as DDT so harmful to wildlife.

Application

The manufacturer's label instructions should

always be followed when using herbicides. It is an offence under the Control of Pesticides Regulations 1986 to use a herbicide in a manner which is not approved. Details of these regulations are available in MAFF Leaflet UL79 *Pesticides: Guide to the New Controls.*

Herbicides for stump treatment are most effective if they are applied to fresh cuts and so it is good practice to apply them immediately after felling the unwanted trees. Moreover, if felling and herbicide application are carried out at different times, it is quite easy for stumps to be missed out simply because they cannot be seen. Another way of missing stumps is to forget which have been treated and which have not. One way around this problem is to add a dye to the herbicide.

As a general rule, no large-scale spraying of herbicides should take place in ancient woodland and herbicides should on no account be used near rare plants. If spray is used, every effort should be made to stop it drifting over neighbouring vegetation. Triclopyr, which can be used to kill stumps is rather volatile and on hot days its vapour appears to have a tendency to drift.

Duration of Activity in Soil

This depends on the herbicide being used. Most of those discussed in the Appendix are soon deactivated in the soil. One exception may be glyphosate (Roundup) which sometimes apparently remains active in the soil for long enough to reduce the regeneration of species in the area treated. To eliminate drift, this herbicide should only be applied directly on to cut stumps or by direct application to foliage, and not by spraying.

Chain-saw Safety

Chain-saws are very dangerous tools and only trained people should use them. Information about training courses can be obtained from the Agricultural Training Board, 32/34 Beckenham Road, Beckenham, Kent BR3

4BP (01 650 4890) and the Forestry Training Council, 231 Corstorphine Road, Edinburgh EH12 7AT (031 334 8083). Sometimes courses are also run by local agricultural colleges.

The Agricultural Training Board through its regional offices arranges two-day courses for people who are not professional foresters. They are free to people who are employed in agriculture or horticulture. The courses deal with chain-saw maintenance, protective clothing, sawing techniques and the felling of trees less than 30cm (12in) in diameter. The Forestry Training Council provides a series of courses throughout the country via approved instructors. Courses can generally be arranged within eight weeks of an initial enquiry. Fees are arranged with the instructor. The courses range from introductions on the use of the chain-saw for inexperienced users, to advanced courses dealing with the treatment of windblown and broken trees.

Squirrels

Grey squirrels can cause considerable damage to broadleaved trees especially beech and sycamore (Kenward et al 1988). A full guide to the different forms of squirrel control is available from the Forestry Commission (Rowe 1980) and a useful guide to the natural history of squirrels is also available (Gurnell 1987). Great care should be taken to avoid damaging the remaining populations of red squirrels and other mammals such as dormice. Although more research is needed, it is known that the use of Warfarin to control grey squirrels may cause unwanted side-effects. It can lead to the secondary poisoning of animals such as weasels which feed on the dead squirrels (Townsend et al 1984). In addition, it can reduce the populations of small mammals such as mice, which in turn reduces the food supply for carnivores in the area around Warfarin hoppers. The Grey Squirrels (Warfarin) Order 1973, contains a list of counties where Warfarin may not be used for grey squirrel control.

Management Guidelines

- Careful management will improve the conservation value of most ancient woods
- Continuity of habitat is important for the survival of many woodland species
- Management should aim to conserve rare species
- Some ancient woods should be set aside for the scientific study of long-term ecological processes
- Non-intervention areas can be designated in ancient woods
- Account should be taken of the possible consequences of natural factors such as fire, gale damage and disease when managing ancient woodland
- Non-native trees should generally be excluded from ancient woodland
- Natural regeneration is the preferred method of restocking ancient woodland
- Planting should be restricted to those parts of ancient woods where planting has taken place before
- It is preferable to restock stands with species of local provenance especially in semi-natural ancient woods
- Increase the amount of old and dead wood
- Leave some dead standing trees but ensure that they are not dangerous
- Simple management plans should be drawn up for ancient woods
- A limited range of chemical herbicides may be used for the control of invasive species and for the spot treatment of weeds around the base of trees planted at wide spacings
- The manufacturer's instructions should always be followed when herbicides are used
- Only trained people should use chainsaws
- Grey squirrels should be kept under control

5   Coppice and
Coppice-with-standards

This chapter considers the management of coppice and coppice-with-standards for nature conservation. The first sections deal with the reintroduction of coppicing; the planning of the coppice rotation and the types of labour available. In the sections that follow, coppicing itself is described, as are the marketing of coppice products; the management of young coppice growth; the creation of new coppice stools and the management of standards.

The Reintroduction of Coppicing
Conservation Value of Coppicing
Worked coppices often have a particularly rich flora and fauna. The repeated cutting of the underwood periodically opens up the canopy which encourages a varied ground flora and provides sheltered open spaces. Coppiced areas can provide good habitat for birds such as the garden warbler and nightingale and butterflies such as the heath fritillary. In addition, the growth of the coppice provides a succession of conditions ranging from open ground with abundant herb development, to dense pole-stage crops suitable for species tolerant of heavy shade. The standards, moreover, provide mature timber habitat and add to the structural variety of the coppice.

Neglected and overgrown coppice has generally lost a lot of habitat variety because of the heavy shade. Some species associated with young coppice growth and rides may have become extinct. Neglect is also likely to lead to changes in the structure of the wood. Where there are species capable of forming large trees, the stand comes increasingly to resemble high forest. The relative proportion of tree species is also likely to change: if a mixture of beech, oak and hazel is neglected for example, the beech is likely to thrive, the oak will hold its own but the hazel coppice may be much reduced. Neglected coppice does have some advantages for conservation and perhaps the most important of these is that it will have a high proportion of dead wood which is of value for a number of species of invertebrates and hole-nesting birds.

The management guidelines for coppice depend on whether the coppice is neglected and out of rotation or managed and in rotation. It is often difficult to decide into which of these categories a piece of woodland should be placed. For simplicity, stands of fifty years' growth, or less, since last cutting can generally be classed as in rotation, but allowance should be made for some species such as lime which sprouts vigorously at any age. Coppice in rotation should as far as possible be maintained as coppice, preferably with an admixture of standard trees, while coppice out of rotation should be promoted to high forest using the species now in the stand and preferably by storing, not replacing, the existing growth.

The Need to Survey
As with all aspects of woodland conservation, it is very important to get to know the woodland well before management is started. As likely as not, coppicing will not have taken place for at least thirty years, and if a wood is being managed specifically for nature conservation a year or two's wait, while its current state is assessed, will do little harm. It is only after woodland surveys

(Above) *In this part of Chaddesley Woods, Worcester-shire, there is dense stocking of oak standards, and the coppice has suffered as a result. If the manager wished to maintain the coppice in this stand, the standards would have to be thinned*

(Below) *The standards are so dense in this area of Garston Wood, in Cranborne Chase, Dorset, that very little of the coppice survives. In this sort of situation, it will probably be best to manage the stand as broadleaved high forest*

(Above) *Large areas of old, overgrown oak coppice are found in the uplands of western Britain. Much of this was grown to provide bark for the tanning industry. This is a characteristic example near Watersmeet, Lynton, Devon. It is often impracticable to coppice these areas today because of grazing pressure and difficulties of access. For the purpose of nature conservation, it is probably best to allow stands like this to develop into high forest*

(Opposite, top) *This stand at Norsey Wood, nr Billericay, Essex comprises sweet chestnut coppice, together with some maturing birch. The coppice shows a single season's growth. Well grown chestnut coppice can be profitable as it provides useful, longlasting fencing material. Sweet chestnut is an introduced species of long standing which is frequently found in ancient woods in southern and eastern England*

(Opposite, below) *This stand of overgrown hazel coppice is in Monk's Wood National Nature Reserve, near Huntingdon, Cambridgeshire. Some larger ash coppice can be seen in the middle distance. There are large areas of hazel coppice in England. It was especially important in the production of the hurdles which were used for seasonal fencing. There is still a market for hazel thatching spars*

have been carried out that the full variations in the habitat are likely to be discovered (see Chapter 3 and Kirby 1988).

Coppice Species

Almost all the native British trees are capable of sprouting new shoots from the cut stumps of established trees. The least vigorous in this respect are beech, gean and birch. Hornbeam can be slow to sprout. Of the native conifers, Scots pine will not coppice, but yew will. Some species, such as wild service and gean send out suckers as well as coppice shoots. Many of the shrubs commonly found in woods, such as dogwood, guelder rose and elder also coppice.

The Age of Coppice Growth

It is sometimes possible to find out when a stand was last coppiced from the detailed records kept by the larger agricultural estates but it is best to treat these records with some caution (see Chapter 2). The records might show, for example, that coppice was last cut in the 1920s, but it is quite possible that further, unrecorded, cutting has taken place especially during the war years. Many woods have no associated estate records and the only sure way to find the age of the coppice poles is to fell some and count the annual rings. This is normally quite simple to do but, sometimes, if the coppice has been suppressed by dense standard trees, the rings are very close together and difficult to decipher. In these cases, it is possible to underestimate the age of the coppice poles. With experience it is relatively easy to give a rough estimate of the age of coppice poles of different species.

Planning the Coppice Rotation

In many parts of the country, coppice woodland was traditionally managed on a form of 'normal rotation'. An estate's woodland would usually consist of a number of woods of varying sizes. The woods were subdivided into falls, ie, small blocks of coppice of the same age. These small blocks have a number of regional names: in Kent, for example,

they are known as cants, while in the north Midlands they are often known as haggs.

Most woods would be made up of a number of different coppice falls, but the smallest woods might consist of a single fall. In general, the area of woodland felled each year roughly equalled the total area of woodland on the estate divided by the length of rotation. Thus if there were 120ha (295 acres) of woodland and the coppice was cut after fifteen years' growth, the average area of coppice felled each year would have been around 8ha (22 acres). In this case, if the av-

A plan of Norwood at Grove in north Nottinghamshire. This has been redrawn from a document in the Nottingham University Manuscripts Department (Ref Ey 513). The plan dates from the late eighteenth century and shows the division of Norwood into 'haggs'. The dates show when underwood was felled. The average length of each rotation was nineteen years. Norwood was cleared during the mid-nineteenth century.

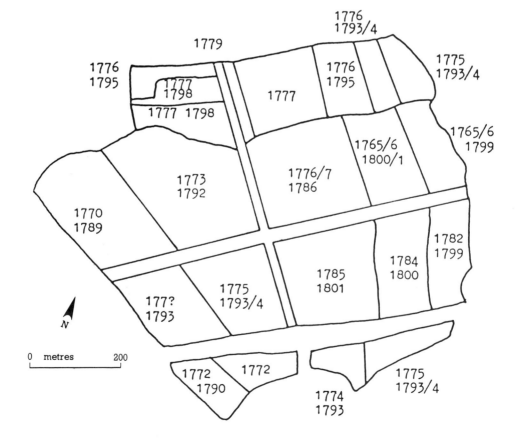

erage area of a fall was 0.5ha (1¼ acres), sixteen separate falls would be coppiced each year.

The advantage of this sort of traditional coppice management for nature conservation is that it results in a wide range of different ages of coppice in most woods. This means that at any one time there will be suitable habitat available for most species. The reintroduction of a traditional coppice system over a whole estate's woodland is usually, however, impracticable: either the estate is broken up, or some of the semi-natural woodland has been lost. Moreover, in terms of nature conservation there is little need to reconstruct the traditional form of management in such detail.

The traditional coppicing regime may be modified to take account of current management aims by, for example:

1 resuming coppicing in only a proportion of the original woodland area;
2 lengthening the rotation;
3 not coppicing every year;
4 altering the size of falls;
5 altering the layout of falls;
6 modifying the distribution of falls within a wood.

Partial Coppicing

There is no need to resume coppicing over the whole of an ancient wood. If only part of a wood is to be coppiced, how is this area

A plan of Ast Wood, near Ledbury in Herefordshire. The term used for the coppice divisions in this part of the country is 'fall'. This plan shows the boundaries of the falls which were used during the latter part of the nineteenth century. They vary in size from just over three to eight acres (1.2–3.2ha). The rotation length at this time varied from twelve to fourteen years. Falls eight and nine were cleared and converted to agricultural land in the early 1970s.

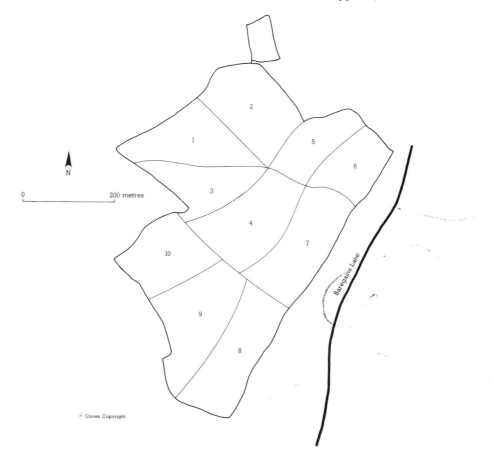

chosen? In general, from the point of view of nature conservation, the youngest coppice should be cut initially as this is most likely to form successful regrowth. The older coppice can be left to increase the structural diversity of the wood, and is in itself beneficial to some species (Sterling and Hambler 1988). On the other hand, if the whole of a wood is to be coppiced, there is a case for tackling the areas consisting of the oldest coppice with a good density of stools first. These areas will produce a greater volume of utilisable firewood than the younger areas and may therefore provide useful income. More importantly in conservation terms, if the coppice is left uncut for a long period, the heavy shade it casts may damage the ground flora. Sometimes the oldest area of coppice has been left uncut for so long that much of its flora may already have been lost. In this sort of situation, however, it is difficult to know how many of the species may survive as seeds in the soil unless some trial coppicing is carried out.

Lengthening the Rotation

The age at which coppice is cut has varied through history and depends on the tree species and the markets for the coppice. Table 3 gives some examples of the age at which different species can be cut and possible products. When coppicing is resumed it may not be possible to recut the coppice after the traditional period. Instead the rotation may be lengthened to say forty years to obtain a reasonable firewood or pulpwood crop. If possible, however, there should always be some areas of young coppice of less than ten years' growth, as many species depend on the early stages of the coppice cycle (Fuller and Warren, in press).

Another factor that may help to determine when coppicing should occur is the age at which the species concerned begin to flower and bear seed. This is important because coppicing can be used as a means of encouraging or discouraging natural regeneration. If the regeneration of small-leaved lime is required, for example, the regrowth of lime coppice should be left long enough for the regrowth to bear seed. Conversely, if, as may be the case with sycamore, regeneration of a species is not required, the coppice must be cut before it reaches flowering age.

It is difficult to give precise ages at which the different tree species begin to produce viable seed as this varies from site to site. Coppice tends to bear seed earlier than maiden trees and most species are able to bear seed after ten to twenty years' growth. The main exceptions are oak, beech and sweet chestnut which need between thirty and forty years' growth (Evans 1984).

Not Coppicing Every Year

If 1ha (2½ acres) is to be coppiced each year, and coppice is felled at thirty years'

Table 3 Coppice: tree species, coppice products and cutting age

species	product	age (years)
alder	turnery	10–20
ash	turnery, thatching sways, tool handles, fencing rails	10–25
birch	turnery, horse jumps	15–25
hazel	thatching spars, pea sticks	6–10
hornbeam	firewood	15–35
lime	turnery	20–25
oak	fencing, tanbark	18–35
sweet chestnut	cleft palings, poles	10–20

(based on Crowther and Evans, 1986, pp6–7)

growth, the total area to be coppiced will have to be at least 30ha (74 acres). If an area smaller than this example is to be coppiced under the same regime, then it may be better to coppice every other year rather than reduce the size of the coupes (felled areas). In small woods with few falls, the interval between successive cuts may be as long as five or ten years.

The Size of Individual Falls

This will depend to a large extent on the resources and labour available. In most cases, areas of less than 1ha (2½ acres) will be coppiced at one time. Contractors generally prefer felling large areas, while if volunteers are used it may only be feasible to coppice areas of around 0.5ha (1¼ acres).

When calculating the area to be felled in a season the area of open ground, such as rides and ponds, which may form part of the coupe should be taken into account. It is also necessary to consider the effects of surrounding woodland on the coppice regrowth. If only a small area of less than 0.25ha (⅔ acre) is cut, and this is surrounded by overgrown coppice, then the growth of the cut coppice may be restricted by the lack of light. Such small coupes may be appropriate, however, in woods of less than 2ha (5 acres), where larger coupes would restrict the potential age range in different falls.

Altering the Layout of Falls

The most straightforward layout is to have rectangular falls at least one edge of which adjoins a ride. This type of pattern was frequently imposed on ancient woods in the eighteenth and nineteenth centuries, but there is no reason in terms of nature conservation why the boundaries of current falls should follow such examples.

There are some occasions where a different layout is preferable. For instance, if only a small area can be coppiced and the bulk of the wood is overgrown coppice then strips of coppice alongside rides should be cut. These must be wide enough to allow sufficient light to enable the species characteris-

tic of woodland rides to thrive (see Chapter 9). In some circumstances an irregular couple layout might be used. If, for example, an area of alder coppice associated with a wet flush has to be treated separately from the surrounding woodland type, then the coupe boundary could follow the irregular boundary of the alder stand.

Distribution of Falls Within a Wood

In the past, the whole of a small wood might be cut in a single season, but from the conservation point of view it would be better to coppice it in at least two stages. With larger woods of over 20ha (50 acres), it may be desirable to fell more than one coupe in a year. This will mean that the different age classes of coppice are better distributed through the whole wood. Care should be taken in deciding the order in which the coppice falls should be cut. As a general rule, adjoining falls should be cut in sequence. This allows the different species which thrive in the light conditions to move from fall to fall around the wood. In addition, the falls should be cut in such a way that any damage caused to coppice regrowth by the removal of coppice poles and timber is reduced to a minimum.

Labour

The four main types of labour used are:

1 commercial;
2 own labour;
3 government-funded schemes and
4 volunteers.

Commercial

Coppice can be sold standing to contractors who carry out the coppicing according to a list of conditions drawn up by the woodland manager. Work specifications for contractors should be drawn up to ensure that the methods used are not harmful to nature conservation. Essex County Council employs contractors for coppicing and includes the following clauses in its contracts:

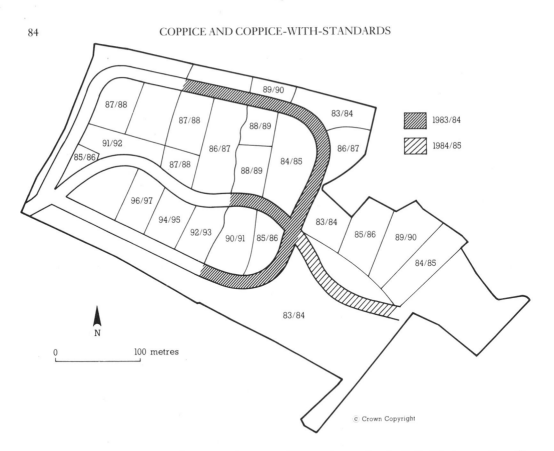

The coppice rotation for Bulls Wood, near Bury St Edmunds, Suffolk. This map shows the planned pattern of coppicing from 1983 to 1997. It also indicates the programme of ride clearance over two seasons

1 Coppice (multi-stemmed) trees to be cut down to the stool and the cut to be angled down to the outside.

2 Maiden and standard trees to be *left* are marked with a silver spot.

3 Undue damage to the rides must be avoided and if necessary carting should be suspended during wet weather. Should the purchaser be unable to meet his commitment to remove the wood before 31 March 199- because of weather conditions, it should be understood that while the council will be as flexible as possible, movement of timber may be suspended during the spring time for reasons of conservation.

4 Brushwood is to be burnt, fire sites should be as few as possible and well away from standing trees and stools.

Often the quality of the coppice is so poor that no market can be found for the poles. This can make it difficult to find a contractor who is willing to do the work. Other forms of labour may have to be considered. Sometimes, however, overgrown coppice contains a mixture of marketable and unmarketable poles. In this case, a possible solution is to let a contractor take out all the wood suitable for specialist markets and then to fell the remaining coppice using estate labour, a firewood contractor or volunteers. This second stage would be carried out at a loss, but it would 'set up' the coppice for the new scheme of coppice management.

Own Labour

If only a small amount of coppicing needs to be done, it may be possible for the woodland manager to do the work or to make use of farm or estate labour. Coppicing is done in the winter months when other farm work is slack but the reduction in the agricultural labour force has made such winter work less important than it once was.

Government-funded Schemes

In recent years a number of coppicing schemes have made use of teams funded by the Manpower Services Commission which was the precursor of the Training Agency. The use of such teams meant that quite extensive coppicing schemes could be carried out. The success of these schemes depended to a large extent on the quality of supervision. With the advent of the Training Agency, the funding of many schemes has come to an end. Some county naturalists' trusts have established their own wildlife management companies to help fill the gap that has been left. These companies may receive payment for training people under the Employment Training Scheme.

Volunteers

Volunteers who are willing to carry out coppicing vary from the inexperienced member of a county conservation trust who turns out occasionally to help, to the trained member of the the British Trust for Conservation Volunteers (BTCV) who has considerable practical experience. The BTCV is organ-ised on a regional basis, but initial enquiries can be addressed to their head office at 36 St Mary's Street, Wallingford, Oxfordshire, OX10 0EU.

The amount of time it takes to coppice an area depends on the quality of the coppice, the tools used and the type of labour available. It varies considerably. Volunteers cannot be expected to work as long hours as contractors.

Coppicing
Timing

It is possible to coppice at almost any time of the year but it is best to cut between October and March. Traditionally there was less other work on the land in this period and it is easier to coppice at this time because of the reduced undergrowth and lack of foliage. It is preferable to stop coppicing after the end of February to ensure that as little damage as possible is done to the emerging ground flora. The bird breeding season, March to July, should also be avoided. Coppice should not be cut in August because this will encourage late summer shoots which will not have time to ripen before the first frosts. One way to extend the traditional coppicing season is to start work in September. This is too late in the year for the development of shoots that

Table 4 The length of time taken to cut and sort coppice in four differing areas in Essex

Area (ha)	coppice age	labour	tools	man days	man days per ha	produce wood tons	poles n
2.8	25	1 ft + vols	chain-saw	120	43	130	5000
0.2	50	vols	chain-saw	c30	c150	14	100
1.6	50	2 con-tractors	chain-saw	50	31	120	–
0.4	60	1 ft + vols	hand saw	50	123	32	100

notes: ft = full time, volunteer man-days are variable

(based on Ranson, *Coppicing and its products* 1979)

would get damaged by frost. An added advantage is that at this time of year the rides are usually dry and the plants growing in the ride will have seeded.

Cutting

The boundary of the area to be felled should be marked clearly by painting crosses on trees at the corners of the coupe. This ensures that the contractors or volunteers doing the work do not mistakenly coppice areas that ought to be left alone. Normally, all the stools and maidens, ie, young seedling trees, within the marked area should be cut. The main exceptions are those stems that are selected as future standards. In addition, it may be

Table 5 Labour and time needed to cut 0.4ha (1 acre) of coppice of different ages

Age of coppice	Number of people	Number of weeks
7 years	1	4
15–20 years	2	3
neglected *c* 50 years	2	2

(Information provided by Suffolk Ancient Woodland Project, 1987)

necessary to avoid coppicing especially rare trees. For example, if only a single wild service tree is present, this might be left uncut so that seed could be collected. Any trees that are to be retained need to be marked clearly with paint.

Traditionally, coppice was cut with axes but there is little reason to use them today. There is some evidence to suggest that the use of blades results in a greater number of shoots than the use of saws but there seems to be no effect on the height that the shoots reach (Phillips 1971). Chain-saws are considerably quicker than axes; hand-saws are considerably safer than either. Whatever the equipment used, it is very important to follow the safety guidelines laid down by the Health

and Safety at Work Act 1974.

The stumps should preferably be left with outward sloping cuts so that water quickly flows off. The main difficulty in felling is the precise positioning of the saw blade so as to maximise the length of pole and yet limit damage to the stool or the, as yet, uncut poles. This can be especially difficult with overgrown hazel coppice because of the density of the stems.

Coppicing is made much easier and safer if all brambles, rose stems and small stems are cleared out of the way of the stool first. Otherwise, they get in the way and cause the saw to jam. Small branches are removed from the cut pole with a bill hook or bow saw. If there are some experienced workers and a larger number of volunteers, the most efficient way of working is for the experienced ones to go on ahead and cut as much coppice as they can, with the less experienced clearing bramble and cleaning, sorting, and carrying the poles.

Removal of Coppice Poles

Care should always be taken to do as little damage as possible to the ground flora when removing coppice poles. One great advantage of coppicing over other forms of managing woodland is that the poles and wood produced are of a size and shape which is relatively easy to handle. Consequently, there is likely to be less damage to the woodland floor during the removal of coppice compared to large timber trees.

The damage caused to rides by heavy loads of coppice on a trailer being pulled by tractor can, however, be considerable. The use of a tractor with an hydraulic box, rather than a trailer, can reduce the amount of damage. As a general rule, existing rides and tracks should be used for the removal of coppice poles and timber. The amount of damage depends on the type of soil: less damage is likely on well-drained sandy soils than heavy clays. If possible loads of coppice should be moved when the ground is hard with frost. After late April the ground may start drying up but, by then, removal of coppice poles will damage the flora of the rides and stands and also disturb birds.

Where extensive coppicing is to be carried out, it may be necessary to modify existing rides with the addition of hard core so that frequent access by wheeled vehicles is possible. If this is done, it is important to consider the damage that may be caused to the existing ride flora (see Chapter 9).

The length of cut poles and the way in which they should be stacked depends on the species concerned, the use to which the poles are to be put and the labour and machinery available. If the coppice produced has a commercial market, the poles should be cut to the length required by the purchaser. The length will often be around 2m (6ft 6in), as this enables the poles to be transported efficiently on lorries.

The most likely market for areas of overgrown mixed coppice is firewood, and in this case the poles should be cut up initially into manageable lengths of about 1.2m (4ft) and then carried to the ride side for stacking. The logs should be stacked on the edge of the ride, just inside the stand, to avoid damage to the ride flora and to reduce access problems. Firewood is generally sold by the tonne or by the cord. The cord is a traditional method of measuring the volume of wood. It is usually defined as a stack of wood 2.44m long by 1.2m high by 1.2m wide (8ft by 4ft by 4ft).

The contents of a cord work out at 3.5 cu m (128 cu ft), but the actual volume of timber is about 2.13 cu m (75 cu ft). This amount of wood weighs 1.57 tonnes after felling, but when it is seasoned it will weigh about 1 tonne (James 1982).

Yields

Yields of coppice are difficult to predict: they vary markedly depending on the age and species of the coppice, the soil type and climate of the the site. Research carried out by the Forestry Commission in the sixties (Begley and Coates 1961) suggested that the annual yield of freshly felled coppice varied from around 3 to 7 tonnes per hectare (2½ acres) (see Table 4). The density of stools per hectare is also an important factor (Crowther and Evans 1986).

Records of coppice yields have been kept by the Ancient Woodland Project of the Suffolk Wildlife Trust over the past few years. These suggest that yields of 14 cords of firewood per acre (54 tonnes per ha, freshly felled) can be expected when coppicing an area of overgrown ash, maple and hazel woodland. The figures also show that the yield varies enormously from species to species. For hazel the yield may be as low as 10 cords per acre (39 tonnes per ha), for elm it is around 30 cords per acre (116 tonnes per ha) while for small-leaved lime it can be as high as 40 cords per acre (155 tonnes per ha).

Table 6 Yields of coppice

Species	Site	Range of average annual increment from two sample plots (tonnes per ha)
ash	Wellesbourne, Warwick	3.0–4.0
lime	Coughton, Warwick	4.1–5.4
birch	Rowlstone, Hereford	4.7–6.5
oak	Penyard, Hereford	4.0–5.9
alder	Shobdon, Hereford	4.4–6.9

(based on Begley and Coates, 1961)

Lop and Top

When the poles have been cut, there is the problem of what to do with the 'lop and top', that is the smaller branches and twigs. In the past this was no problem: the twigs and branches were bundled together to form faggots for fuel. Nowadays, not even the most enthusiastic woodland historian or ecologist wants to spend hours doing this job, so alternative ways of getting rid of lop and top have to be found. The two main ways are to leave it to rot on the site, or to burn it.

The easiest way to deal with lop and top is simply to leave it to rot. This can also be the most desirable method from the point of view of nature conservation. Decaying branches provide dead-wood habitat for a number of invertebrates and help to increase the number and diversity of species living in a wood, although this value is limited by the small size of the material. If the lop and top is simply left where it falls when the coppice is cut, it is then difficult to get around the site to cut stools or remove poles. It can also be unsightly and spoil the view for visitors who have come to look at the coppicing and its associated flora. One way around this problem is to make piles of lop and top, or to gather it together in rows. Piles are more appropriate for the heavier branches. They provide good dead-wood habitat for invertebrates, but they also enrich the soil and may thus encourage plants such as nettles. Piles may take over forty years to break down and should not be placed on rare plants or where where they will interfere with coppicing. Rows are better for brushwood. They leave bands of clear ground and are less unsightly than leaving the material where it falls.

Lop and top may actually be useful. It can be used to make dead hedges around areas of recently cut coppice in order to protect the coppice stools from grazing animals. More simply, it can be piled on top of the cut stools to deter browsing by deer (see Chapter 8). If a shredding machine is available, the unwanted material can be shredded and taken away as fuel, or used as a mulch.

Disposal of lop and top by burning should be avoided if possible. Fire damages the field layer and may also damage nearby stools or standards. It will also modify the soil. Sometimes, however, the sheer quantity of material makes burning necessary. If so, fires should never be made under or near standard trees and should be placed as far as possible from coppice stools. Fires should not be allowed to spread, otherwise they may destroy too great an area of the ground flora. The number of fires should be minimised, with no more than three or four per 0.5ha (1¼ acres). If possible, when the area is recoppiced the sites of previous fires should be reused in order to limit the effects of fire.

Table 7 Types of produce and prices from coppice

Item	species	specification	price (1985)
fencing stakes	oak, ash	1.6m (8cm top diam) peeled and pointed	80p
hedging stakes	any	1.6m (4cm diameter) pointed	£8/100
heatherings	most	3m (2.5cm diameter)	£2.5/20
bean poles	any	2.7m (4cm diameter)	£1.5/15
pea sticks	any	1.2m fan	50p/20
tree stakes	any	2m (6cm diameter)	50p
firewood	any	logged	£30/tonne

(from the Woodland Trust, 1986)

In addition to lop and top there are waste products such as saw dust or bark peelings. These are usually in too small quantities to cause any damage but large piles of sawdust should be kept away from sites with rare flowers.

Marketing Coppice

The markets for coppice produce depend on its quality and vary from region to region. Table 3 gives some examples of possible markets for species of different ages. The most widespread markets are firewood, fencing material and wood pulp. The only significant specialist market at present is that for chestnut palings and posts which is concentrated in Kent and Sussex (Rollinson and Evans 1987). There are, however, some small-scale markets for specialist products such as hazel thatching spars.

The wide variety of products that can be made from a single wood is shown in Table 4 which is based on the Woodland Trust's Pepper Wood in Worcestershire. This is the Trust's first 'community woodland' and it has been found that there has been sufficient demand for all the produce which the volunteers have created (Woodland Trust 1986). Only a limited amount of effort was put into advertising; most products have either been sold to volunteers themselves, or their contacts. Most purchasers have collected the produce themselves.

Several local projects have been set up in recent years to help with the marketing of woodland produce. Silvanus (1987), which is based in Devon and Cornwall, aims to encourage the management of woodland in co-operation with existing advice services. The project helps owners with the measurement, presentation and sale of woodland produce and it is planned to initiate the management of 25,000ha (62,000 acres) of small farm woods in the Westcountry over a ten-year period. In Suffolk, the Ancient Woodland Project of the Suffolk Wildlife Trust has been established to help with the marketing of coppice products. It also helps with the management of

six nature reserves and twenty-five privately owned ancient woods.

Management of Young Growth
Coppice Growth

One of the characteristics of coppice is the rapid growth of stems from the cut stools, especially in the first two growing seasons. Goat willow will frequently grow over 2m (6ft 6in) in the first season and ash may grow well over 1m (3ft 3in). This growth is almost always considerably faster than the growth from transplants, even if these are planted in tree shelters. Because coppice stools have established root systems, there is usually no need to weed the ground around the stools after coppicing. Long-neglected coppice may show less vigour than regularly cut coppice but this is by no means always the case.

Thinning

There is generally no need to thin coppice stems during the rotation. Thinning improves the yield of the remaining poles, but tends to reduce the total yield per hectare (Harris 1956). It is not generally done now because of the large amount of extra work involved. If left alone, the shoots tend to thin themselves through competition for light and space. The only reason to thin the coppice shoots today is if the manager requires to grow especially good-quality poles of species such as ash and chestnut on a long rotation of say thirty years.

Elm Coppice

Despite Dutch elm disease, elm should generally be coppiced along with the other species. It is not known what the long-term effects of this disease on the distribution of elms will be but, in parts of the country which were first affected by the disease, vigorous shoots, originating from the stool or as suckers, are now around twenty years old. There is some evidence that the beetle which spreads the disease is not attracted to young growth and so one way of ensuring the survival of the stools is to coppice them regularly at less than ten years' growth (Brasier and Webber

Dense brambles growing in Bigsweir Wood, Gloucestershire. Strongly growing brambles can suppress coppice regrowth, and may also compete with naturally regenerated or planted trees. Where the problem is serious, the bramble may have to be brought under control. However, account should also be taken of the benefits that brambles bring as an important food plant for butterflies, bees and small mammals, and as useful cover for game and nesting sites for birds.

small mammals and provides many nesting sites for birds. In addition, ancient woods are very important sites for the study of the distribution of different sub-species of bramble (Edees and Newton 1988). However, dense bramble, which is a partial evergreen, can suppress the field layer as much as overgrown coppice (Mason and Long 1987). This problem seems to have become worse since the decline in the rabbit population in the fifties (Kirby 1979). The dense growth may smother coppice stools, especially if the regrowth is frequently browsed by deer, although it can also have the effect of protecting regrowth from deer. It also competes with any naturally regenerated or planted trees.

If there is a reasonable density of stools, with inter-stool distances of between 5m and 10m (5½yd to 11yd), there is little need for bramble control. Where there are gaps in the pattern of stools, it may be necessary to control the spread of dense brambles. This can be done by cutting or applying herbicide.

Cutting should be repeated each year until the coppice shoots have grown up out of danger. In areas of coppice this normally has to be done by hand because the irregular distribution of stools makes it difficult to use tractor-mounted cutters. Although the most effective time to cut is probably May and June, this time should be avoided because of nesting birds. The best time to cut the brambles back in nature conservation terms is normally autumn or winter.

The best herbicide for controlling brambles is glyphosate (see Chapter 4 and the Appendix). Note, however, that glyphosate also kills most broadleaved species: its use must be limited to the area around the coppice shoots to be released from the bramble and care should be taken to avoid damage to broadleaved herbs.

1987). On the other hand, it appears that the disease is losing some of its vigour, at least in southern Britain (Rackham 1989), and there is a case for simply coppicing the elm at the same time as the other trees in the stand and not to give it special treatment.

Coppicing and Brambles
Coppicing may result in a dense growth of impenetrable bramble, which benefits from the full sunlight. Bramble has some value for nature and game conservation: it is an important food plant for butterflies, bees and

Protection from Grazing
Grazing can curtail coppice regrowth. Methods of controlling grazing in woods in general are discussed in Chapter 8, but specific problems associated with coppice are discussed

here. The main offenders are usually deer and rabbits: they are much more difficult to fence out of a recently coppiced area than stock, although sheep cause much damage in upland areas.

Browsing by deer is one of the most serious problems facing coppice woodlands, especially in the south and east. Richard Prior has written extensively on the subject of trees and deer, and readers are referred to his books (Prior 1968, 1983, 1987). The precautions necessary in the case of deer depend on the size of the local deer population. If it is low, the simplest method is to place brash (cut branches) around or over the cut stumps, but this is only successful with light browsing.

Another method is the construction of dead hedges made from unwanted coppiced material. At Hilly Wood in Cambridgeshire, for example, a dead hedge 480m (525yd) long and 2m (6ft 6in) high was recently made around a coppiced area of 1.4ha (3½ acres). The hedge was constructed by hand, and the lop and top was laid at a 45° angle. The contractor charged £1 per metre, and the job was grant-aided by the county council and the Countryside Commission. The dead hedge kept deer out of the coppiced area for twelve months and this allowed the coppice to grow above browsing height.

Deer prefer to eat certain species of tree. This means that in the long term, deer browsing not only results in a reduced yield and the death of some stools, it also causes the increase of some tree species and the decline of others. In Hayley Wood, Cambridgeshire, for example, the order of preference is ash, sallow, hawthorn, hazel, maple and aspen (Rackham 1975). In Lady Park Wood, Gloucestershire, during the forties and fifties, there was a rather different order of preference. For the main tree species it was oak, ash, beech and birch, while for subsidiary species it was dogwood, holly, maple, hazel and sallow (Peterken and Jones 1989).

At Bowdown Wood near Newbury, the preference of deer for sallow and ash means that the future of these species is in some jeopardy and special measures are being taken to protect them. It is possible to fence individual stools to prevent browsing, but this is very expensive and is only suitable if a particularly large, old stool needs protection. In some woods the browsing is so intense that there is hardly any point in coppicing. In the long term the only way to reduce the problem is to control the deer population. The alternative is to consider converting the coppice to high forest by storing, or to introduce pollarding (see Chapter 8).

Rabbits can also cause a lot of damage. In some areas, such as parts of the Yorkshire Dales, the rabbit damage is so severe that expensive rabbit-proof fencing may be the only way of protecting coppice regrowth.

Creating New Coppice Stools

There are several circumstances where a manager may wish to establish new stools. Old coppice stools die and leave gaps. Overgrown stools may blow over in gales. The regrowth from felled standard trees is sometimes weak and short-lived. The existing growth may contain unwanted species such as rhododendron which when removed will leave gaps. New stools can be provided by cutting existing maiden saplings, layering and planting. None of these methods will be effective if the gaps are not free of overhanging growth from adjoining stools and standards.

The simplest method is to cut naturally regenerated saplings at the same time as the rest of the crop. The cut stump will produce a number of new shoots. This is the cheapest method, but it gives the manager little control over which species become new stools. It is the preferred method for nature conservation because it helps to maintain the genetic diversity of the coppice.

Layering is a means of increasing the number of coppice stools by vegetative reproduction. It involves bending down a stem from a coppice stool and pegging it into position. This should be done when an area is

being coppiced and before the sap begins to rise in March. Selected stems are partly cut through at the base, as in hedge laying, and positioned in a shallow trench. Side shoots are removed. The stem is pegged down at about 1m (3ft 3in) intervals and the soil alongside the stem is firmed down. Stems should not be layered next to paths, otherwise people will tend to trip over them and they will be pulled out of the ground. When the stem has rooted, it can be dug up and planted where required. Shoots and roots develop along the partially buried stem and weeding may be necessary to allow this new growth to succeed. Eventually, a separate coppice stool develops. This method can only be used if gaps are available next to coppice individuals of the desired species. One of its advantages is that the layers are able to withstand periods of drought. Appropriate species are hazel, sweet chestnut and lime, but the method does work with others.

The third method of filling gaps is to plant individuals in the gaps. The resulting seedlings can be cut at the next coppicing. This enables the manager to make large

One way of increasing the number of coppice stools is to layer selected stems. Here, hazel is being pegged down at Monks Wood, Cambridgeshire. Overgrown ash coppice which has been singled or 'stored' can be seen in the background

changes in the composition of the coppice and is thus least desirable for nature conservation. The planting of species already found adjoining the gap is rather more acceptable, especially if the plants are of local origin. Self-sown seedlings of species such as ash and field maple are often available. Planting is likely to be most acceptable in the areas of coppice made up of a single species such as the extensive areas of hazel coppice in southern England and other places where the distribution of coppice stools has been greatly influenced by past planting.

Standards
Standard trees greatly enlarge the range of available habitats and create a mature structure. The retention of some old trees is very important as they provide habitats for species such as woodpeckers and the purple

hairstreak butterfly which could not survive in areas of pure coppice. Standards may also provide timber of commercial value.

The number of standards per hectare has varied dramatically through history and from estate to estate. Standards were often felled at irregular intervals subject to demand. Rackham (1980), for example, considers that in many woods the density of standards increased substantially in the late eighteenth and nineteenth centuries. Many woods today have more standards than is good for the coppice. In addition, many woods have suffered from having the best and most valuable stems creamed off, leaving only those standards with a poor form. Although these trees are not commercially valuable, they are important for nature conservation, and at least five should be retained per hectare until some newer standards have aged. Old trees are also often found along the boundaries of woods and wherever possible these should also be retained. The management of pollards is discussed in Chapter 8.

Species

By far the most usual standard is one of the two species of oak. The other species frequently grown in this way is ash but most other native broadleaved trees, including lime, field maple, wych elm, hornbeam and cherry can be grown as standards. The main exception is beech which casts too much shade for the successful growth of coppice underneath.

There is no reason why some species which have not traditionally been grown as standards, such as some of the willows and birches, should not be allowed to grow as standards for nature conservation purposes. These trees will produce dead-wood habitat much more quickly than oak or ash.

Felling

In a properly managed coppice, standards should be grown until they reach marketable size, which now usually means between 90 and 120 years, or at at least three to six coppice rotations. As a result of past neglect, many surviving standards are much older than this. Some of these over-mature trees should be retained indefinitely because they provide useful old-wood habitat. Additional standards should be allowed to mature before old standards are felled.

To avoid damage to growing coppice, and to ease the removal of timber, any fellings of mature standards, and thinnings, should coincide with the felling of the surrounding coppice. The felling of standard trees requires considerable skill and expertise and only trained foresters should be employed for this purpose.

Density of Standards

The number of standards may vary from thirty to one hundred per hectare (see Table 8). At the higher figure, the standards would be about 10m (11yd) apart if evenly spaced and could only be tolerated with the coppice if most were very young. The table shows how at any one time there should be a number of different generations of standards (Evans 1984). Each of the four generations shown takes up about 10 per cent of the area.

As the density of standards increases there is a greater chance that the coppice growth

Table 8 Number of standards per hectare and their age

Age (years)	1–20	21–40	41–60	61–120
coppice rotation	1	2–3	3–4	4–6
no of stems per ha	50	30	13	7
% of area occupied	10	10	10	10

(based on Evans, 1984, p80)

will be suppressed. A general rule that can be applied for conservation coppicing is that standards should take up about a third of the woodland canopy area. If standards are widely spaced they are able to develop large crowns and hence grow rapidly in diameter as with free-grown oak (Jobling and Pearce 1977).

Distribution

Traditionally, standards were scattered throughout a stand. An acceptable alternative is to grow the standards in small groups situated within a matrix of coppice. Possible advantages of this method are that it can be easier to obtain better quality standard trees and that it increases the area of coppice which is not shaded by standard trees.

New Standards

In an established stand of coppice-with-

A general view of mixed coppice at Bradfield Woods in Suffolk. Here there is a low density of standards and the coppice shows vigorous growth. In the foreground are some hazel stools; the larger stools in the middle distance are ash

standards, new standards are required to replace any that have been felled. In stands of pure coppice, new standards can be created to benefit conservation. Standards can be derived from natural regeneration, stored coppice or transplants.

When an area is coppiced, a selection of any young seedling trees (maidens) should be left uncut so that they can develop as standards. For every hectare (2½ acres) of coppice, there should be at least fifty young standards of less than twenty years' age. The use of tree shelters can greatly assist the growth of young standards.

If there are not enough young trees, it may be necessary to thin some coppice stools down to one stem and allow them to develop into standard trees. This method is known as storing and it is discussed below in the section on the conversion of coppice to high forest.

In many stands there is a general lack of oak natural regeneration, and in cases where no suitable stems are available for selection when the coppice is felled, it may be necessary to plant some oak saplings if this species is required. These should preferably be of local provenance and be planted at wide spacings. Where grazing is not a problem, oaks can be established by planting acorns. At Monks Wood, Cambridgeshire, when acorns were planted at the same time as the hazel coppice was felled, the growth of the young oaks was found to keep up with that of the surrounding hazel coppice (Steele and Welch, 1973).

Pruning

The growth of the surrounding coppice should nurse the standards to form good straight stems. One problem with oak standards, however, is that they tend to form epicormic shoots, ie shoots that sprout from the tree trunk, in the season following coppicing. This is especially likely when overgrown coppice is felled. The epicormic shoots provide good nesting sites and are beneficial to invertebrates but if high-quality oak timber is to be produced they have to be pruned off. To be successful, this pruning should take place regularly in June and August, before the shoots from the preceding periods of growth have become woody (Evans 1987).

Conversion of Coppice to High Forest

In some woods, the restoration of coppicing is not appropriate for nature conservation purposes. This is especially true of the large areas of overgrown oak coppice in the south-west, Wales and Scotland which were formerly grown to supply bark for the tanning

This stand of overgrown oak coppice at Coed Rheidol in Dyfed is characteristic of the large areas of such coppice found in western Britain. Many of these woods are important sites for mosses, ferns and lichens. From the point of view of nature conservation, there is little reason to start coppicing this sort of woodland

industry. In other woods it may not be feasible to reinstate coppicing: the density of stools may be too sparse to make coppicing worthwhile; there may not be sufficient labour to maintain a coppice cycle.

From the nature conservation point of view, the best way to deal with this sort of overgrown coppice is to convert it to high forest by storing. This entails the retention of a single well-grown stem from a coppice stool while the remainder of stems are felled. If there are some good stems in the overgrown coppice, the cost of storing should be covered by the sale of produce and there may be some profit. Storing should preferably result in an even spread of stems over the stand. For nature conservation, the stools selected to be stored should lead to as great a variety of species and ages of tree as possible. If there are any significant gaps, natural regeneration may be encouraged to fill them or they can be retained as woodland glades.

One of the main drawbacks with storing an area of ancient coppice is that the traditional management is disrupted. This means that the historical and cultural interest in the site may be devalued and the species that have fitted in with the coppice cycle over the centuries may be adversely affected. Storing is not, however, necessarily a one-way process and it may be possible after a transitional stage of high forest management to restore the coppice when the crop is felled.

Storing is not an appropriate technique for all species of tree. Hazel coppice, of course, will not grow into timber, while stored hornbeam is likely to die. If ash coppice is stored, the resultant standards often have fungal infections which reduce the value of the timber. Oak is the most commonly stored tree. Another problem with storing is the quality of the selected stems. It is sometimes quite difficult to find enough good straight stems, many will be curved as a result of growing from a stool. In addition, there is a tendency for the base of the selected stems to rot. This means that the singled stem may not be windfirm and can lead to the death of stools.

Management guidelines

- If coppice is of less than fifty years' growth, retain in coppice rotation, preferably keeping as close as possible to traditional rotation length
- When coppicing is resumed, rotations should be less than twenty-five years if possible, but may be extended up to forty years if this is necessary in order to satisfy markets such as firewood
- Aim for a normal age-class distribution of coppice growth or at least a wide spread of age classes
- Retain or develop standards over a normal age span: ensure both the retention of older trees and a succession of young standards
- Renew both the underwood and standards by natural regeneration or vegetative propagation, not planting
- Planting if necessary, should be restricted to standards and locally native species

- Although standards are often maiden oaks, they can be developed from promoted stool growth and include individuals of other species, such as ash and birch, already in the wood
- If coppice is of over fifty years' growth, whenever feasible, select and thin the stand in order to develop a high forest canopy from the original standards and stored underwood
- If coppice is of over fifty years' growth, resume coppicing in at least part of the stand, preferably strips adjacent to the rides (see also Chapter 9)
- When storing, the thinning intensity depends on the characteristics of the stand
- When storing, if there are any old trees, they should be retained as standards and kept free of overhead and side shade

6 Broadleaved High Forest on Ancient Sites

The main ways in which ancient broadleaved high forest has originated are by:

1 stored or singled coppice, often containing some older standards if the woodland was previously coppice with standards, on ancient sites;
2 natural regeneration after a previous crop has been felled on ancient sites. Birch high forest is a particularly common and distinctive type in the Highlands;
3 broadleaved plantations made on ancient sites.

These three processes do not necessarily take place separately and stands of broadleaved high forest in ancient woods often contain some trees which originated as stored coppice, some which have naturally regenerated and some which have been planted.

As with other types of ancient woodland, there is no single correct way to manage this type of woodland from the conservation point of view. The individual woods vary dramatically in origin, in the management that they have had in the past and in the amount of money that can be usefully spent on their management today. Moreover, the ideal treatment of a stand for nature conservation is often very different to that which would be carried out if commercial timber production was the sole aim.

Silvicultural Systems
A silvicultural system is the process by which crops of trees '. . . are tended, removed, and replaced by new crops' (Troup 1928). In broadleaved high forest on ancient sites the best silvicultural system to apply from the point of view of conservation is usually some form of 'group system'. This is the system which is most likely to result in diverse woodland structure with trees of all ages within the same stand.

It also allows for considerable continuity both in terms of selected individual trees and woodland structure. In this book, group systems are defined as silvicultural systems where the unit of management is 0.5ha (1¼ acres) or less in area. Different people give different names to the various types of group system. The classification used here is that of Pryor and Savill (1986) who consider that there are three types of group system: group felling; group shelterwood and group selection.

Group Felling
This is the simplest method: a stand is subdivided into groups of even-aged trees and all the trees in this group will be felled at the same time. Although each group is even aged, groups of different ages will be present in the same stand.

Group Shelterwood
This is a system where an overstorey of trees is retained in order to provide shelter for the young crop growing in the same group. For a time, therefore, there will be trees at two stages of development. Once the young crop has reached mid-rotation, however, the old trees will have been felled and from this time to maturity, the group will be even aged.

This fine stand of beech is at Bradenham Woods in Buckinghamshire. The high density of trees casts a heavy shade, and there are few shrubs. Such pure stands of beech are the result of careful management of natural regeneration over many years. Some of the Chiltern beechwoods might be improved in terms of nature conservation by planting some additional species such as field maple or gean, which are native to the area, but which are unlikely to regenerate naturally

Group Selection

This entails the division of a stand into groups each of which, for a large part of its life, is uneven aged. Emphasis is placed on getting successful regeneration in the groups, rather than scattered evenly throughout the stand.

These three systems are model systems. In practice a number of permutations and combinations of approaches are likely to be used under differing circumstances. Group shelterwood and group selection are the ones which most closely follow the likely structure of natural temperate broadleaved woodland (Jones 1945). The group felling system, on the other hand, is the easiest of the three to operate and to some extent mimics the small groups of clear-felled woodland which are a characteristic of coppice management.

Clear felling should not generally be used in stands of ancient semi-natural woodland but is an important form of management in areas of planted ancient woodland. In this guide it is defined as the felling of all trees within stands greater than 0.5ha (1¼ acres) at the same time. The main disadvantages for nature conservation include the lack of continuity between the old crop and the new, the lack of old trees and the general uniformity of the resulting stands.

Age Ranges

For most woods it is preferable for nature conservation purposes to have a range of age classes. The ideal for large woods, or for groups of smaller woods under the same management, is to modify the stand structure so that a wide range of stands of different ages is always present. This allows for continuity of habitat, and, moreover, allows a wider range of species to exist than in a wood made up of stands all of the same age.

Taking birds as an example, some, such as yellowhammmers and greenfinches, prefer fairly open areas, or young growth; another group, including nightingales and blackcaps, is associated with dense woody growth, such as maturing coppice or trees at the thicket stage; while woodpeckers and pied flycatchers are usually found in mature woodland. Having trees of different age within a stand is also important: buzzards, for example, like to survey prey from large old trees (Smart and Andrews 1985).

The idea of a 'normal' forest, in which all age classes are present 'in those proportions which, for the given area of the wood and chosen length of rotation, will maintain the existing age distribution of stands indefinitely' (Peterken 1981) is well established in commercial forestry. In the case of large areas of woodland, a normal range of age classes should be beneficial in commercial terms. It is likely to reduce the risk of damage by disease, wind or animals at any one time and lead to a regular annual supply of timber. The concept is less frequently applied to individual woods as there are considerable economic disadvantages in having a wide range of different aged trees within the same wood.

Many woods today contain a high proportion of over-mature stands, the result of decades of neglect. In order to achieve a full range of different aged stands it may be necessary to space out the felling and restocking over a longer period than can be justified commercially. Some stands should be retained as over-mature while others, especially the poorer ones, may have to be felled before they are mature.

There are some cases where the felling and restocking of even-aged woods to increase the age range is not necessarily the best course of action for nature conservation. Some mature and over-mature woods, though even aged, may contain, for example, important lichen or invertebrate communities which can only be maintained on mature trees. Such stands are likely to be less common and less re-creatable than any young stands which replace them: if all the mature trees were felled at once, species which depend on them will die out and are unlikely to return. In addition, if even aged woods are left unmanaged, some trees will eventually die, natural regeneration will ensue and the age structure will become more diverse without any intervention.

Rotation

In broadleaved high forest on ancient sites, the length of rotation should be as long as possible in order to obtain mature timber habitat, allow the development of a shrub layer and, possibly, advance natural regeneration. In many cases, a compromise will have to be reached between the commercial need for trees to be felled at their economic maturity and the conservation need for long rotations. The length of time it takes a tree to reach economic maturity depends on its species, the quality of the site and the eventual use to which the wood is to be put. In most cases a tree's economic maturity occurs long before it reaches its biological maturity. Thus ash may achieve economic maturity after 65 years, while it does not become over-mature in any biological sense until it is 150 or more years old; an oak might achieve economic maturity at 120 years, but will probably not reach the end of its natural life span for another 200 years or more.

Retention of Old Trees

Whenever a stand is felled it is desirable to allow a few of the trees to grow on indefinitely either as individuals scattered among younger trees or in an area which will in the future be treated as a separate stand. If an area is open to the public, care must be taken that any old trees retained are not in a dangerous condition. The importance of retaining a proportion of old trees cannot be over-emphasised. It has been estimated that nearly a third of all woodland bird species require holes for nesting (Smart and Andrews 1985). During the winter old trees provide roosting sites for many small birds, places where bats and other small mammals can hibernate and suitable habitat for many invertebrates.

Tree Species and Restocking

In areas of ancient woodland that have been planted in the past, there is, in nature conservation terms, a need to retain the native species now on the site, but not necessarily in the virtual monocultures that may be present. Thus, areas of pure beech could be restocked with beech and a mixture of other locally native trees such as oak, ash and gean. Similarly, oakwoods could be restocked with oak but other species such as birch, rowan or holly should be allowed to come in.

Tree Species and Silvicultural Systems

The species composition will, to some extent, determine which silvicultural systems may be used. Group selection, for instance, is only possible where the natural regeneration is shade bearing. Species such as ash and beech are able to tolerate shade for a few years but need full overhead light after that (Evans 1984). Oak restocking demands reasonably large clear-felled areas: certainly not less than 0.5ha (1¼ acres).

Conversion to Coppice

When timber trees are felled there is often coppice regrowth. This can be seen from the many areas of multiple-stemmed trees which have resulted from the untended regrowth of broadleaved plantations felled in World War II. In addition there are large areas of high forest which originated as stored coppice. Although it would be possible to start coppicing

these areas, there is likely to be less advantage for nature conservation in doing this, compared to the restoration of coppicing in areas that have not been converted to high forest. This is because the flora and fauna which flourishes under coppicing conditions are likely to have already deteriorated, or never existed. It is therefore better to concentrate on the coppicing of areas which have been coppiced in the past fifty years or so. There is no reason, however, why coppicing such areas for demonstration purposes, or just to see what happens, should not be done as long as account is taken of the need to leave sufficient old-wood habitat.

Felling

Where to Start

The pattern of felling to be carried out depends on the silvicultural system which is being used, the age of the crop concerned, the accessibility of the stand and the demand for different types of timber. For nature conservation purposes, it is best *not* to start with felling the oldest trees in a wood. The reason for this is that old trees are relatively scarce and it is easier, and quicker, to have some old trees in a wood by keeping those already there than by waiting for other trees to reach a great age. It is therefore better to retain some of the oldest trees and to start felling those trees which are just reaching economic maturity.

Coupes

As a general rule, the smaller the coupe, the better it is for nature conservation. The size of coupes, under the different silvicultural systems, has been outlined on p97–8. By definition, clear felling involves felling areas of more than 0.5ha (1¼ acres) at once as smaller areas would be classed as 'group felling'.

The proportion of a wood being felled at one time is also an important consideration. Kirby (1984b) has suggested that the maximum proportion of a wood which should be clear felled at any one time lies in the range of 10–20 per cent of the area in any 5–10 year period. Taking the lowest proportion in this range (10 per cent every 10 years) the whole of a 10ha (25 acre) wood would take 100 years to replace, with 1ha (2½ acres) being felled every 10 years. The highest rate of change (20 per cent every 5 years) would result in a 10ha (25 acre) wood being felled and restocked in 25 years.

The location of felling coupes is usually determined by the age, size and quality of the stands of timber in a wood. In some cases, however, especially in a large wood where stands are of an even age, there is considerable choice as to where the coupes should be made. This can be a difficult decision, as there are conservation arguments for both felling adjoining coupes in succession and dispersing the coupes throughout the wood.

The advantage of cutting adjoining coupes in successive years is that this will ease the spread of species which like light conditions from one coupe to another. On the other hand, such a method of felling and restocking may perpetuate the even-aged nature of the wood as it can result in a gradual increase in age from one end of the wood to the other.

One way round this problem is to arrange the coupes in a circle or spiral in such a way that adjoining coupes can be felled in successive seasons and yet at the same time ensuring that coupes of different ages can be found next to each other. This will result in a varied wood and enable the existence of transitional zones between mature high forest and young trees (Harris 1984).

Avoiding Damage to the Remaining Crop

Felling mature trees under the different group systems is rather more difficult than when clear felling. Special care must be taken not to damage any of the maturing trees or the young regeneration. This means that harvesting is generally more time-consuming and expensive.

Avoiding Damage to Rides

Managing woodland as broadleaved high forest results in the production of many large trees and this can lead to problems when the time comes for removing the timber. In particular there can be considerable damage to the ride flora by the heavy equipment used in extraction. It should be noted that group systems are likely to result in more use of rides than a single fell.

It is often difficult to avoid some damage to the rides when removing timber and if substantial damage does not happen regularly the ride flora often recovers remarkably quickly. It is best to take steps to reduce the damage, however, and the simplest of these is to avoid the removal of timber when the soil is very wet. This is especially true in clay areas where extraction of felled timber may have to wait until the ground is dry (see Chapter 9).

Timing

Felling of broadleaved trees traditionally takes place in the winter months before the sap rises and this is also the best time of year for nature conservation. Felling in the autumn and winter means that there is less lop and top foliage to deal with and that there is less likelihood of damage to the surrounding vegetation. It is especially important to avoid felling during the bird breeding season between March and July.

Natural Regeneration
Tree Species

One advantage of natural regeneration is that it tends to maintain the semi-natural species composition of the wood (see Chapter 4). Not all of the native trees regenerate freely, however, and hence the species composition may alter. Those from which natural regeneration is most likely to be successful are ash, birch and Scots pine (for details about the native pinewoods see Chapter 7). Beech and oak can also be grown successfully by this method, but because good seed or 'mast' years for these species tend to be at intervals of between 7 and 10 years, there is a considerable risk of failure (Evans 1988). Skill is needed to manage the seed trees in such a way as to maximise the supply of seeds at the correct time. In addition management plans have to be flexible enough to take advantage of particularly good seed years, as with acorns in 1976, and this can be difficult.

Non-native and Non-local Species

Although natural regeneration is a good method of encouraging the survival of the semi-natural characteristics of ancient woodland, in some circumstances, as with the regeneration of larch, Corsican pine or sycamore, the regeneration although natural will not consist solely of native trees. Moreover, native trees which are not indigenous to the locality in question may regenerate freely. What should be done about these trees which are in the wrong place in nature conservation terms? The treatment depends to a large extent on the characteristics of the different species concerned (see Chapter 4).

The two exotic species most likely to regenerate freely in broadleaved ancient woodland are rhododendron and sycamore. Rhododendron should be controlled or eliminated. It is very attractive in flower but it obliterates the ground vegetation. In addition it spreads so effectively that it can greatly increase the costs of any management (Tabbush and Williamson 1987).

Sycamore is widespread and not particularly rich for wildlife. It regenerates easily and the timber is valuable (Taylor 1985). The treatment for sycamore depends on how much of it there is, and how long it has been in the stand. If there is little sycamore, and natural regeneration is just beginning, then it is probably worthwhile trying to eliminate it.

If sycamore is a species of long standing, and present in moderate quantities, it should not be allowed to dominate the stand although it would be difficult to eliminate it totally. Where it is already dominant, it should probably be accepted as such, as more harm may be caused to the remaining semi-natural

features of the wood by removing the sycamore than by leaving it alone.

Encouraging Natural Regeneration

If a good supply of seed is available, the next requirement is a suitable seed-bed, preferably with some exposed mineral soil. It can be an advantage to break up the soil surface and vegetation by lightly harrowing but this can, of course, be damaging to the ground flora. Increased germination can also be encouraged by the disturbance of the ground associated with felling and removing timber and by the use of mechanical screefers. As with the use of a harrow, both these methods cause damage. Very successful regeneration of oak at Windsor (Pryor and Savill 1986) was brought about by actually rotovating the acorns into the ground but this treatment would damage the existing ground flora in many ancient woods. Birds, voles and mice cause serious problems by taking seeds and their control may be undesirable in nature conservation terms.

Advance Regeneration

Advance regeneration is natural regeneration which grows in a stand before the current mature crop is felled. Its occurrence is one indication that an area is likely to be suitable for the use of natural regeneration.

Regeneration established before the onset of felling should be retained since it hastens the establishment of a new crop and generates structural diversity in the next stand. The retention of such advance regeneration is one of the characteristics of the group shelterwood management system.

Management of Young Growth

One of the advantages of using natural regeneration is that there is usually no need to weed between the young trees. If the overstorey is thinned carefully while regeneration is taking place, the growth of weeds may be restricted by the shade cast by the remaining mature trees. It is unlikely there will be any flush of ground flora. At this stage it is also critical, however, to ensure that there is enough light to encourage the growth of seedling trees. It may take up to ten years to achieve a reasonable stocking using natural regeneration and, after this time, the crop may be less dense than if planted at standard forestry spacings.

When natural regeneration is carried out on a small scale, it may be possible to use tree shelters to protect individual seedlings of good quality. These reduce the need for rabbit fencing. Once the seedlings become established, they may need protection from grazing animals such as deer (see Chapter 8).

Treatment of Mature Trees

For the purposes of conservation, it is preferable to remove the mature trees in a number of stages, rather than all at once. This allows the development of a stand containing trees of different ages. If good regeneration is expected, it is possible to fell about half the mature trees in the autumn and winter following the production of the seed. The remaining trees will help to restrict the growth of competing vegetation and reduce the extent to which soil moisture increases due to reduced transpiration.

Many of these remaining trees can be felled as the natural regeneration develops, but around four to five per hectare (2½ acres) should be retained in order to provide old-tree habitats. When the mature trees are felled, care should be taken to do as little damage as possible to the regeneration.

Crop Variation

Natural regeneration usually results in a more varied crop in terms of composition, age and tree density than a planted crop. Another advantage for nature conservation is that it tends to result in a distribution of species which reflects natural site variations within the stand.

The relative proportions of species in the natural regeneration may not be exactly the same as that in the previous crop. Upland oak woods, for example, usually contain a higher proportion of birch and rowan in the regeneration than in the existing canopy (Kirby 1984b). This increased variation is beneficial for nature conservation but can lead to problems for foresters. The lack of control as to which species regenerate; the possible regeneration of large numbers of less valuable trees such as birch or alder; and the lack of uniformity over the stand all lead to increased management costs. However, although the regeneration may be very mixed, if there are enough of the required species to form the final crop, these can be promoted by thinning the less commercial species.

Planting
Distribution of Species

One problem with planting from the nature conservation point of view is that the distribution of different tree species over the site is entirely unnatural. It depends on the planter and does not reflect natural variations in the site. This situation can be tempered when planting by the careful choice of species to mimic obvious site variations, but the resulting variation is likely to be less subtle than that resulting from natural regeneration.

Provenance of Trees

Planted trees are almost always of a different provenance to the previous crop (see Chapter 4) and may be of a different species. Indeed, from the forester's point of view this is one of the main advantages of planting: it is possible to introduce trees of a provenance or species which are likely to produce a greater economic return than the existing trees. For nature conservation, however, this means that the new crop will have almost no continuity with the current semi-natural trees and shrubs.

One way of reducing the adverse effects of planting is to plant species and provenances native to the site. This is especially important in ancient woods which retain an essentially semi-natural distribution of species. If possible seed should be collected from the trees already growing in the stand (Beckett and Beckett 1979). Often natural seedlings are found growing in glades or rides within a wood where they are not required. For small-scale plantings these can be dug up and moved to the position required, but this is an uncertain and expensive way of obtaining trees of local provenance.

Mixtures of Broadleaves

The loss of variety often brought about by planting can be reduced by using mixtures of appropriate broadleaved species rather than planting a whole stand with a single species. In general, inter-mixed blocks of nine or more trees of the same species are easier to manage than rows of mixed species. Alternating bands made up of three rows of the same species are also easier to manage, but in hilly areas this method produces a characteristic 'pyjama stripe' pattern which is very obvious in the landscape.

Although conifers provide a useful source of income relatively early in the rotation, they should not be used as a nurse crop in ancient woodlands because of the damage that they cause to the ground flora. In the rare cases where a nurse crop is considered essential, in order to improve the form of the planted trees, broadleaved species such as birch should be used although these may not provide as much protection from side winds and frost as conifers. Where nurse crops are used, it is important to ensure that they do not come to dominate the final crop.

Spacing

If possible, a matrix of semi-natural woodland should be retained around relatively small planted areas and within the planted areas, natural regeneration should be encouraged. If an even planting scheme is preferred, it is a good idea to reduce planting density. In commercial forestry it is usual to plant from 2,500 to 4,000 trees per hectare (2½ acres). This means that the trees are between 1.5m and 2m (5ft and 6ft 6in) apart. For nature conservation a lower density of about 400 planted trees per hectare (2½ acres) is preferred.

This results in a slower canopy closure than denser plantings and this provides space for natural regeneration to enter. The natural regeneration will nurse the planted trees and may provide free additions to the potential timber growing stock.

One problem with the wide spacings approach is that the Forestry Commission does not consider areas with less than 1,100 trees per hectare (2½ acres), with trees at 3m (10ft) spacings, to be 'adequately stocked' and such planting would not normally receive grant aid. It is possible, however, for groups of trees to receive grant aid on a pro rata basis, as long as the spacings within the group are at least 3m (10ft). In addition, natural regeneration in between planted trees can contribute to the overall stocking and this may bring it to the required 3m (10ft) spacing.

Tree Shelters

Wide-spaced planting has been encouraged in recent years by the development of tree shelters which increase the growth rate of the planted trees and provide partial protection from grazing animals. Recent research has shown that growth rates within tree shelters increase substantially when the bottom of the shelter is sealed by being partially buried in the soil. This is thought to be due to the consequent increase in the level of carbon dioxide within the shelter (Frearson and Weiss 1987). The only broadleaved species which should not be protected by a tree shelter is beech which seems to be particularly susceptible to the beech woolly aphid (*Phyllaphis fugi*) when grown in this way (Potter 1987).

Apart from their beneficial effects on growth rates, tree shelters are also a way of keeping track of the exact position of planted trees which can otherwise be difficult to find amongst the surrounding vegetation. Indeed, in some cases the trees are too easily identifiable and the use of shelters can lead to problems of vandalism. A further advantage of tree shelters is that they can be a means of protecting young trees from deer damage (see Chapter 8). One of their few disadvantages is that some forms of shelter act as traps for small mammals and birds. A number have now been designed to reduce the risk of this occurring.

Management of Established Trees
Weeding
The three main types of weeding are by hand, by machine and by using chemical weedkillers. All types of weeding are made much easier if the trees to be weeded are easily identifiable. One of the advantages of planting over natural regeneration is that trees can be planted in rows which makes them easy to find. However, with the advent of tree shelters, selected natural regeneration, or widely spaced planted trees, can be very obviously marked.

Weeding by hand is the best method for nature conservation but is expensive in terms of labour. If small areas have been restocked, or if only a small number of trees scattered throughout a stand need weeding, then it can also be the most efficient method. Mechanical weeding is normally restricted to areas that have been planted up in rows.

Chemical weedkillers are the most frequently used form of control because they are both cheap and effective (see Chapter 4 and the Appendix). They are more effective than either hand or mechanical weeding because they reduce root competition. Unfortunately they have a direct and harmful effect on the nature conservation value of a site: the flora of the area treated is either totally destroyed or heavily modified. Some chemicals, such as those designed to be used in conifer plantations, destroy not only the weeds but also any young broadleaved natural regeneration that happens to be growing in the area. If chemical control has to be used, it is best to use spot treatments of no more than a 1m (3ft 3in) square around the young trees. This reduces any long-term effect on the flora of the stand as a whole, especially if wide-spaced planting has been used. Coppice regrowth should not be treated with chemicals. In addition to the three standard methods, for small numbers of

trees, it is possible to keep the ground around the base of the young trees free of weeds by using some form of artificial mulch such as a square of black plastic.

Cleaning Young Plantations
When the young crop begins to close its canopy and reaches the pole or thicket stage, it is frequently necessary to make room for the trees which are to form the final crop by clearing the surrounding woody vegetation. This is known as cleaning. Apart from the benefit it brings to the selected trees, this process also opens up the stand and makes it easier to mark for thinning and to carry out ecological surveys. Unfortunately, if cleaning is taken too far, it can have a harmful effect on the nature conservation value of a piece of woodland. This is especially so if it entails the felling of coppice regrowth or natural regeneration. If it is wished to produce trees with high-quality stems, however, it will be essential to remove any trees which are a direct threat to the final crop trees and to free them from the growth of climbers such as honeysuckle and clematis.

Pruning
The aim of pruning is to achieve as long a lower bole without branches as possible, in order to reduce the number of knots in the timber. Pruning is especially important in the production of high-quality tree trunks which are destined to be used for the production of veneers. Such timber can fetch very good prices.

Pruning is more likely to be required for trees which have been established at a wide spacing. As it is an expensive and labour-intensive operation it is only applied to the final crop trees. In general, pruning should be started early on and the smaller the branches are when they are removed the better.

Lopping
This is a type of pruning which involves the removal of large branches from an established tree. It is not essentially a silvicultural

operation but is used to lessen the possible nuisance that a tree might cause. Common examples are the removal of branches from roadside trees which block the line of sight at a junction, the removal of old branches which pose a threat to people and the pruning of branches from trees growing near to power lines.

Lopping is different from pollarding in that it does not normally involve the removal of all the branches on a regular rotation to produce a crop of poles (see Chapter 8). When lopping is carried out, the branches should, if possible, be left to rot on the ground in shade near the tree in order to increase the amount of dead-wood habitat.

Thinning

Thinning involves the manipulation of the number of trees in a stand over the life of a crop of trees to improve the quality of the final crop trees. If possible, those trees which are not destined to form part of the final crop are removed when they have reached a saleable age. Recommended thinning re-gimes for different crops are available from the Forestry Commission (Rollinson 1985). The timing of thinning in broadleaved high forest depends on how fast the trees grow and how closely they were originally stocked.

As a general rule, on ancient sites, thinning should be as early as possible as the increased light allows the development of the ground and shrub layers. The very heavy thinning associated with the management of oak using free-growth techniques can also be advantageous in nature conservation terms (Jobling and Pearce 1977). Unfortunately, however, it is often unprofitable to make early thinnings in the short term because there is currently little market for the small-sized produce.

It is common practice to remove dead or dying trees while thinning a stand. However, this reduces the dead-wood habitat, and wherever possible, the dead trees should be left to rot standing, or at least left to rot on the ground within the stand (see Chapter 4). The exceptions to this rule are trees suffering from a disease which may spread from the dying trees.

Management Guidelines

- Diversify the age class structure of stands and allow some stands to grow beyond their economic maturity
- Develop a mixed age structure by means of adopting some form of 'group system' by encouraging advance regeneration wherever practicable and by having a diversity of systems within one wood
- Keep felling coupes small
- Have a conservative approach to the choice of tree species, keeping those already there and emphasising local native species
- Use as much natural regeneration as possible
- The spread of additional species of local native trees into the wood should be allowed
- Self-sown stock should be retained with planted stock in order to diversify the canopy structure and composition

- Existing dominant native species should remain as a significant component of the stand
- Native broadleaves should be included in new stock
- Diversity of stand age should be encouraged by restocking over an extended period. In large woods aim to keep to a normal age spread
- Diversity of species to be encouraged by varied planting on varied soils as appropriate
- Make use of wide-spaced planting nursed by natural growth
- Make use of free growth of oak where appropriate
- Thinnings to be as early and heavy as practicable

7 Coniferous and Mixed High Forest on Ancient Sites

Two very different kinds of ancient woodland are dealt with in this chapter. The first section discusses the management for nature conservation of coniferous plantations which have been made on ancient woodland sites. The second section describes the management of the remaining native pinewoods of Scotland.

Conifer Plantations on Ancient Broadleaved Sites
Origins
Although a stand of trees may have been planted only forty years ago, the wood is still classed as ancient if the ground on which the trees were planted has carried trees for at least 400 years. It is the *site* which is ancient, not the trees. From the late nineteenth century onwards there has been a trend towards the planting of coniferous trees on ancient woodland sites. This reached a peak between the mid-fifties and the mid-seventies.

The proportion of conifers in a stand can range from a scatter of trees, perhaps the remnants of unsuccessful underplanting, through a variety of different types of mixture to virtually pure stands of conifers. As the proportion of conifers varies, so does the stand's current conservation value and the best form of management to improve this. In general, the greater the proportion of conifers, the less the current conservation value of the stand.

The Effects of Planting Conifers
The best way to see the effects of planting conifers in woodland is to visit an ancient wood which has stands that have been planted and

stands which remain in their original state. There is often a dramatic contrast between the two types of stand especially if the conifers have reached the pole stage when they cast an especially dense shade. This all-year-round shade, together with the mat of dead needles which usually collects on the floor of the wood, heavily modifies the conditions within the stand.

The full ecological effects of the introduction of pure crops of conifers on to an ancient woodland site are difficult to assess (Mitchell and Kirby 1989). One reason for this is that as most of this type of planting is fairly recent any resultant ecological changes are likely to be still in progress. It is clear, nevertheless that, in the short term at least, many of the effects are damaging to wildlife and natural features.

The main problems resulting from planting conifers on ancient sites are:

1 The loss of semi-natural trees and shrubs due to the planting of conifers. The conifers tend to shade out many native trees and shrubs and others will be removed in the course of the forestry operation known as 'cleaning'. Native trees and shrubs may, however, survive on the margins and will rarely be eliminated totally. Such trees may be important for nature conservation: Waring (1988) has shown, for example, the importance of remnant broadleaves for the moth population at Bernwood in Oxfordshire.

2 A reduction in the ground vegetation in terms of both the number of species and the quantity of individual plants. This

is largely due to the heavy shade cast by most conifers, particularly during the thicket stage when the ground flora may be almost completely eliminated. This, in turn, affects the fauna that depends on the ground vegetation. The ground vegetation increases as the plantation approaches maturity and grows luxuriantly when the conifers are eventually felled. In the meantime, however, the populations of dormant seed in the soil may have been greatly reduced (Harris and Kent 1987).

3 The build-up of acid, or humus owing to the nature of the falling needles, although this may in part be a cyclical process with much of the litter being broken down again upon clear felling.
4 A reduction in the amount of mature timber habitat. Although this is not a necessary consequence of planting conifers, it usually accompanies this process.

The worst stands for conservation are those made up purely of conifers, particularly spruce or hemlock. Pure planting was especially in vogue from 1955–75 and so many stands of pure conifers on ancient sites are 15–35 years old at the time of writing. Most of these stands were established with the aim of a softwood timber yield, usually on a rotation of 50–60 years.

Although there is no doubt that, on balance, conifers have an adverse effect when planted on ancient sites, there are some positive aspects. One of these is that prior to canopy closure young stands of conifers, like broadleaves, may provide abundant ground vegetation, shrubs and temporary open space which is a valuable habitat for butterflies, birds and flowering plants.

Surviving Broadleaved Trees in Stands of Conifers

Although an area may have been planted up with conifers, it is highly likely that some broadleaved trees will continue to survive in the stand. Indeed, there are many instances where conifer crops on ancient sites, even if originally intended to be pure, contain some broadleaved trees. Surviving broadleaved trees may have originated in a number of ways:

1 because trees were retained from the previous crop, usually to reduce the impact of the felling on the landscape;
2 through natural coppice regrowth or natural regeneration which has not been completely cleaned out;
3 because a few broadleaved trees were planted with the conifers, or
4 due to the failure of the broadleaved element of a mixed planting. Thus if a stand was replanted with 50 per cent conifers and 50 per cent broadleaves, and half the broadleaves failed, the remaining crop would be coniferous with 25 per cent stocking of broadleaves.

The Importance of Surviving Broadleaves

If any of the remaining broadleaved trees survive from the original semi-natural woodland, or have naturally regenerated, then they are valuable from the point of view of conservation. Any trees that have been retained from the previous crop are important because they add structural diversity to the stand and provide habitats associated with old trees. Surviving natural regrowth is also important. In some cases there can be a considerable amount of coppice regrowth or natural regeneration in stands that are supposed to be pure conifers.

The success of this sort of regrowth has often dogged foresters trying to obtain pure stands. In 1949 Hammond noted that when making plantations in old hardwood areas all foresters 'will be troubled with coppice shoots. It is remarkable the vigour that such stools can show.' Hammond made a study of coppice regrowth, and found that it was usually necessary to cut off the regrowth for at least five successive years before the stool was killed, and even then some survived (Hammond 1949). No wonder some wood-

---

Management Guidelines

- The long-term aim should be to return to broadleaved woodland as soon as practicable

- Conifers should be thinned heavily as early as possible in order to encourage shrub and ground layer species. The conifer element should certainly be reduced to less than 50 per cent of the stock by year 40, and below 20 per cent of the stock by year 50

- Semi-natural growth, both maiden and coppice, should be retained as part of the mixture, especially where it is capable of developing into timber trees

- The final crop of conifers should be felled as soon as possible

- Restocking should be by natural regeneration or planting native broadleaved trees, retaining as much self-sown and coppice regrowth as possible

- When restocking, the aim should be a broadleaved final crop

- Conifers may form up to 25 per cent of stocking but only where coniferous, or mixed stands, grew before.

---

land managers simply gave up trying to get rid of the coppice and accepted a proportion of broadleaves.

The survival of such stools is very important for conservation because it means that relics of the semi-natural woody vegetation will survive and, in addition, it will be more likely that areas of the ground flora will remain relatively undamaged.

Treatment of Conifers

Since the instigation of the Forestry Commission's broadleaved policy in 1985, there is less chance that new pure stands of conifers will be planted on ancient sites. However, the guidelines do state that 'conifer woods on [ancient] sites may be replaced by conifers' (Forestry Commission, 1985). From the nature conservation point of view it is much better to replace such conifers with broadleaves.

It has become increasingly clear that, although the planting of conifers in ancient woodland often has a drastic effect on the ground flora, in some woods the semi-natural vegetation has shown surprising resilience. There is every reason, therefore, *not* to consider such woods as a totally lost cause in terms of nature conservation but instead to carry out management to restore the woodland to its semi-natural state.

Conifer Removal

The age at which the conifers should be removed varies from stand to stand depending on such factors as the nature conservation value of the ground flora, the proportion of conifers and the commercial market for the conifers. If, for example, conservation is the main management aim and there is a relatively high proportion of surviving natural vegetation, then the conifers should be thinned heavily or removed altogether as soon as possible.

If, on the other hand, the flora is not of much interest, and there is little surviving semi-natural vegetation, then it is probably a good idea to retain the conifers until they can be sold for a reasonable price. It is not necessary to remove absolutely every conifer. A few individuals, or in a large wood a small stand, will act as a feature to represent a particular phase of a wood's history. If left to grow beyond economic maturity, they will show how conifers develop in old age and may provide mature wood habitat and nesting sites for large birds of prey.

Conifers Forming Less Than 80 per cent of the Canopy

If it is intended to keep on the conifer element of a mixed woodland until economic maturity, it is very important to ensure that the quicker growing conifers do not overtop the broadleaved trees and suppress them. The stand will need to be thinned regularly to ensure that this does not happen. Some conifers are likely to cause more damage to broadleaves than others. In particular, larch and pine, because of their rapid crown growth and branching structure, are more likely to damage adjoining broadleaved trees if thinning is delayed than more upright species such as Norway spruce or western red cedar. On the other hand, as pine and larch let more light reach the woodland floor, they are likely to cause less damage to the ground flora.

Conifers Forming More Than 80 per cent of the Canopy

Where there is a very successful take of conifers, there should be early thinning in order to let as much light on to the woodland floor as possible. This will enable the ground flora to begin to recover. The density of conifers should be kept as low as possible by frequent thinning. Special care should be taken to retain any coppice regrowth or natural regeneration of native tree species.

Native Pinewoods of Scotland

By far the most important coniferous woodlands in Britain for conservation purposes are the native pinewoods of Scotland. Steven and Carlisle (1959) describe thirty-five main sites which have some native pine woodland, and these are thought to cover today, in broad terms, about 11,965ha (29,565 acres) (Bain 1987). If only the better stocked stands of pine are counted, then the total area falls to as low as 5,815ha (14,369 acres).

The surviving fragments vary tremendously in size from the tiny Glen Avon, which had only twenty-nine trees in 1987, to much larger sites, such as Rothiemurchus which covers about 1,539ha (3,800 acres). All these woods are the modified remnants of the natural pine woodland but they do not consist solely of pines. The other frequently found trees are the two native species of birch, aspen, rowan, willow, bird cherry and, along the streamsides, alder.

Apart from the obvious fact that they contain pines, pinewoods differ from other ancient woodland in a number of ways. Some types of management recommended for other types of wood are clearly inappropriate. As a result, the management of pinewoods is dealt with here in a separate section. The most obvious difference is that Scots pine does not coppice. This may be a reason why the native pinewoods have more of a feel of the untouched primeval forest about them than most other ancient woods. Other important differences relate to the methods that can be used to encourage natural regeneration. Pine stands regenerate from seed following disturbance of the site by fire, wind or other agency and the conservation ideal consequently leans towards non-intervention policies. However, it is important not to over-emphasise these differences. The general management prescriptions for these woods, such as a preference for the use of natural regeneration rather than planting as a means of restocking a stand, are equally applicable to these pine woodlands as they are to ancient broadleaved woods.

Minimal Management

The general management aims for conservation purposes have been outlined by Forster and Morris (1977). They suggest that the pinewoods should be allowed to develop with a minimum of interference. This is because even though they have been much affected by human activity in the past, they still remain less disturbed than most other types of woodland in Britain. The minimal management approach is also recommended because the needs of many of the species which live in pinewoods are not known and some management practices may have unknown adverse effects.

The best way forward is to encourage the development of woodland influenced largely by the natural factors such as soil, topography and climate rather than by direct management. In some cases, however, the effects of past human activity are so great, as with the effects of high grazing pressure, that it may be necessary to help these natural processes along. Various methods are discussed in the following sections.

Zoning of Pinewoods

Under the Native Pinewood Grant Scheme it is possible to obtain special rates of grant aid for the natural regeneration and planting of native pine woodland. Under this scheme the woodland is placed into one or more of the following four zones (Bain, 1987):

1 *Conservation zone*: no management allowed except fencing.
2 *Regeneration zone*: no planting allowed. Thinning and selective felling may be used to encourage natural regeneration.
3 *Extension zone*: planting of Scots pine of local provenance allowed.
4 *Buffer zone*: normal commercial forestry may be carried out. If Scots pine is used it must be of local origin.

Natural Regeneration

When the classic study of the native pinewoods was written in the fifties (Steven and Carlisle 1959) the authors noted that most of the trees were over a hundred years old and that there had been little natural regeneration for a century. The main reason for this state of affairs was that most of the woods had been subject to intensive grazing by deer. The other factors that can inhibit natural regeneration are the lack of a large enough seed supply; the lack of suitable soil in which the seed can germinate and the presence of too much shade and competition from other trees or plants. Scots pine seedlings do not grow fast and are not tolerant of shading or root competition. It is a pioneer species which regenerates and grows well on sites such as forest roads, gravel pits and river banks. The provision of correct site conditions is therefore an important means of improving the rate of natural regeneration.

Recent research on stand development in a fenced site at the Black Wood of Rannoch (Peterken and Stace 1987) has shown that natural regeneration is sufficient to allow for continuity. There has been a considerable increase in the number of established trees since 1948 and the older trees are not dying rapidly. This raises the question as to how far it is necessary to encourage natural regeneration in the native pinewoods. It is likely that the original natural pinewoods would have been made up of relatively even-aged groups of trees which would not regenerate until the stand was disturbed in some way (such as by fire or windthrow) or died off from old age. Thus, as long as excessive grazing is controlled, there is no need to worry unduly if there is a lack of regeneration in a dense stand of pine. Also, there would naturally be areas of ground where conditions were too wet or rocky for dense stands of trees to survive, and where a light canopy of pines might be expected.

There is plenty of evidence that pinewoods have oscillated in size in the past and that areas of open heather are natural components of the woodland. Natural regeneration should not, therefore, be artificially encouraged in native pinewoods where conservation is an important objective. Ground preparation may, however, be a useful technique where there is a much reduced population of parent trees, or where the production of a commercial crop is the paramount aim.

Seed Supply

As in many tree species, the number of seeds produced each year varies considerably. Research carried out in the Black Wood of Rannoch (McIntosh and Henman 1981) showed that over a five-year period, production of seed was prolific in two years, but almost non-existent in the other three. The reasons for such variation are not known, but climatic factors are likely to be important. The heaviest seed fall took place in May and June and as might be expected, the quantity of seeds produced was closely related to the number of parent trees. In the two years when large amounts of seed were produced, the average amount falling was 300 seeds per square metre, although the amount of viable seeds varied from 201 per square metre in one year to 102 in the other. The results of this study suggest that sufficient quantities of viable seed were being produced to enable adequate regeneration.

Encouragement of Scots Pine Regeneration

Natural regeneration should only be encouraged artificially if a commercial profit is required. Scots pine regeneration depends, to some extent, on the disturbance caused by tree felling and removal, windthrow and fire. These processes all produce a soil that is unencumbered with the vegetation which would otherwise compete with, and probably kill, any seedling pines that happened to germinate.

What is the most efficient way of copying these 'natural' means of ground disturbance? There is no point in going to the expense of ground preparation if there is not going to be a good crop of seeds that year. The ground preparation must be done before the seed fall in a good seed year. This is not usually a problem, however, as the quantity of seed can be estimated from the young pine cones at least nine months before the seed fall in May and June (Edwards 1981).

Cutting down or spraying competing vegetation with herbicide will not necessarily result in any increased germination because the ground layer has not been disturbed. Burning the vegetation might be considered but this is difficult to tie in with good seed years as the surface of the burnt area may only be suitable for the germination of seedlings a year or two after the fire. Some commentators, such as Forster and Morris (1977) think it could be worthwhile to simulate natural conditions by burning small areas of heather moorland next to stands of native pinewoods.

Another way to encourage regeneration is to remove the ground layer of vegetation and break up the surface of the humus lay-

er of relatively small patches of land where the regeneration is required. This process is known as 'screefing', and can be done by hand with a mattock or with a rotovator. The best size for these areas depends on the situation, and the amount of labour and time available. The areas must be kept in scale with the total size of the wood. Edwards (1981) suggests that for freely drained sites, areas of 20–25 sq m (24–30 sq yd) are suitable, while in wetter areas on peat, plots could be less than 10 sq m (12 sq yd). With smaller areas than this, the competing vegetation may be able to re-establish itself too quickly. Bain (1987) notes that screefing is not necessary on many sites because heavy grazing in the past has kept potential competing vegetation below the height at which pine regeneration is severely limited.

Increasing the Size of Woods by Regeneration

Unlike the ancient woods characteristic of lowland Britain, the ancient pinewoods do not necessarily have fixed boundaries; the boundaries change as some areas of woodland deteriorate and others regenerate. Under natural conditions, therefore, the pinewoods would tend to shift as regeneration took place along their margins. It is good management practice to allow this spread of the pinewoods. Marginal areas, which at present have no trees, should be included in any conservation plan (Carlisle 1977). In some cases, the woods migrate gradually eastwards as the prevailing wind blows the seed in that direction.

Density of Natural Regeneration

Regeneration is not always dense in the first instance, and there is some evidence that regeneration occurs in waves (Dunlop 1983). The first wave may result in a stocking of around 20 per cent, and then, in following years this stocking slowly increases. In the Black Wood of Rannoch, research has shown that the phase of regeneration which started after 1945 was due to 'sustained recruitment over decades, rather than a major flush in one particularly good year' (Peterken and Stace 1987).

Other Tree Species

A number of non-coniferous trees are commonly found in the native pinewoods and there is some evidence that the proportion of these trees has become reduced through human activity. O'Sullivan (1977) considers that nature conservation policies should make some provision for the restoration of this diversity. Areas of the native broadleaved trees (birch, rowan, aspen, alder and willow) growing within the pinewoods should be retained and allowed to regenerate naturally.

Tree Planting

The density of trees produced by natural regeneration may be low in commercial forestry terms but it should not be artificially increased because this results in an unnatural pattern and density of trees. Moreover, the planted trees have limited genetic variation compared to natural regeneration and the gene stocks that survive are not necessarily those that would have survived with natural regeneration.

The nature conservation value of the native pinewoods is based on the fact that each generation has descended from the previous one by means of natural regeneration. This is one of the main distinguishing features between the native pinewoods and plantations of Scots pine (Faulkner 1977). It is not, therefore, acceptable to plant Scots pine in these ancient woods in order to conserve them. It is, on the other hand, possible to plant Scots pine in areas near to the ancient pinewoods, provided only seed of local provenance is used and enough room is left

Deer fencing at Kinveachy Wood, Inverness-shire has allowed the natural regeneration of Scots pine. No regeneration can be seen outside the fenced enclosure in the background, nearer the mature Scots pine

on the margins of the ancient pinewood for the original trees to spread by natural regeneration. Planting of exotic trees and native trees not characteristic of the area reduces the nature conservation value of the pinewoods.

Grazing

General recommendations about fencing are dealt with in Chapter 8. Fencing out the grazing animals is expensive and should be seen as a short-term measure for preserving threatened stands. For larger areas it is necessary to reduce the total grazing population, usually of wintering red deer, by culling but this is likely to reduce the sporting value of land.

Browsing

Although pines can be browsed at any time of the year, they are most likely to be damaged in the winter when there is less other vegetation for the deer to eat (Fenton 1985). If individual trees are lightly browsed, they can develop a new leading shoot but repeated browsing over a number of years is likely to cause the death of the trees. Experiments show that it is the young pine trees below 2m (6ft 6in) in height that are especially prone to damage by red deer (Cummins and Miller 1982; Mitchell, McCowan and Willcox 1982), but heavy snowfall can enable the deer to reach higher than this in the winter. There is some evidence that young pines of below 75cm (2ft 6in) in height are also less prone to damage, but this is only because they are sheltered by the surrounding vegetation. They are likely to be browsed as soon as they begin to grow above this height.

The density of pines is also an important factor. If a young pine tree is isolated, it is much more likely to be damaged than if it is growing together with other pines in a clump. The evidence suggests that once an area of pine regeneration has reached a height of 2.5m (8ft 3in), the damage by deer is more likely to affect the form and rate of growth of individual trees rather than threaten the viability of the whole group. Thus it may be

possible to allow grazing in any such areas of pine regeneration that have become established and the subsequent browsing may even add to the structural diversity of the stand. Indeed, this grazing might also help the germination of seedlings, as the exclusion of deer results in increased competition from plants such as *Deschampsia flexuosa* (Edwards 1981).

The total exclusion of grazing may even prevent regeneration of pine (Dunlop 1975) and lead to the domination of the site by birch and rowan. It must be borne in mind, however, that the growth of any new generation of pine seedlings would be halted by the grazing. The most efficient time to fence an area would appear to be when the seedlings have reached the stage when regular browsing keeps them in check, and the fence needs to remain until the trees have grown to at least 2.5m (8ft 3in).

Mature Trees

If it is decided to manage an area of native pinewood for timber production, the best form of silvicultural method to apply for conservation purposes is likely to be some form of shelterwood system. The stand concerned should be divided up into groups of relatively even-aged trees. When the time comes to fell a group, the majority of trees are felled, but an overstorey of about eighty seed-bearing trees per ha (2½ acres) is left behind (Steven and Carlisle 1959).

The process of felling and extracting the majority of mature trees should disturb the soil enough to provide suitable conditions in which the seeds can germinate. Moreover, the removal of a large proportion of the group means that there is enough light for the new seedlings (Dunlop 1983). The remaining mature trees will provide some shelter for the first ten years or so of the young seedlings' lives. In addition, it is important to leave a proportion of old trees and dead wood in each group as these provide the essential habitat for a number of species including a rich beetle fauna (Hunter 1977).

Management Guidelines

- Native pinewoods should be allowed to develop with the minimum of interference
- The larger native pinewoods should be divided into four management zones: conservation; regeneration; extension and buffer
- Excessive grazing should be controlled so that natural regeneration is able to grow
- Where nature conservation is an important objective, natural regeneration should not be encouraged artificially
- If the production of timber is important, shelterwood is probably the most suitable silvicultural system

- Native pinewoods should be allowed to spread by natural regeneration on to adjoining land
- Native broadleaved trees growing within pinewoods should be allowed to regenerate
- It is not acceptable to plant Scots pine within native pinewoods
- Planting of trees of local provenance near ancient pinewoods is acceptable as long as enough room is left for the original wood to spread by natural regeneration

8   Grazed Woodland

This chapter considers the treatment of ancient woodland where grazing is a dominant factor affecting its conservation value. Aspects of grazing specific to certain woodland types, such as coppice and the ancient pinewoods, are discussed in the chapters dealing with those types of woodland. Guidelines for the management of pollards are also included in this chapter.

Types of Grazed Woodland

Most woods are subject to some grazing and browsing, whether by undomesticated animals, such as rabbits, hares and deer, or by domesticated (and sometimes feral) animals such as sheep, cattle, pigs or horses. Grazed woodland is therefore very variable in type and difficult to classify. One way to consider this problem is to divide woodland, where grazing is a dominant factor, into categories dependent upon its historical development. Harding and Rose (1986) have defined four categories on this basis:

1 The remnants of medieval forests and chases. There are not many of these but most are very important for conservation and some are very extensive. Examples include parts of the New Forest (which is considered to be the largest remaining area of wood pasture in West Europe), Windsor Park, Epping Forest and Hatfield Forest (Rackham 1989, Tubbs 1986)

2 A diverse group of parks, including remnants of medieval parks and parks of more recent origin which may include trees which pre-date the formation of the park. Examples include Moccas Park in Herefordshire, Bradfield Park in Leicestershire and Dalkeith Old Wood in Midlothian (Fairbairn 1972, Fenton 1941). Lists of English parks have been compiled by Cantor (1979), while Scottish parks are dealt with by Gilbert (1979).

3 Wooded commons of medieval origin, which are most frequent in southern Britain, such as the Mens in Sussex (Tittensor 1978).

4 Winter-grazed woods which are used for shelter and grazing by stock which in the summer graze the nearby moors. These are usually found in the uplands (DART 1983).

An additional category is formed by woodlands which are grazed, often throughout the year, in the lowlands. This is not a common practice but does take place where a wood adjoins a pasture field whose boundary by accident or design is not stockproof. This form of grazing is sometimes a preliminary stage in the clearance of the wood (Watkins 1984b).

Nature Conservation Value of Grazed Woodland

It is very important that grazed woodland of long standing, especially the surviving royal forests, and medieval parks and commons (types 1, 2 and 3) should be maintained and conserved. This is not only because of their ecological interest, but also because of their historical importance as cultural landscapes (Rackham 1989). Such woods and parks frequently contain large, old trees which were often pollarded in the past. These are

of considerable conservation importance as they support a large number of invertebrates and lichens.

In contrast, many of the upland woods which are used for winter grazing (type 4) were traditionally managed for coppice, and grazing is not generally of long standing. An exception is the Horner and Hawkcombe group of woods which is one of the main wintering grounds for deer from Exmoor (Harding and Rose 1986). In the past such coppice woods were often grazed once the coppice regrowth had reached an age where browsing would not cause damage. Such grazing may even have helped the coppice regrowth by stopping the growth of bramble from becoming too dominant.

In practice, however, the combination of grazing and coppice often caused damage which led to disputes between the owners of the stock and the owners of the coppice. At present, it is most unusual for stock to be

An example of lowland grazing. New Forest ponies grazing near Bishops Dyke. A recent study indicated that grazing pressure in the New Forest affects the whole ecological shape and functioning of the New Forest system (Putnam 1986)

managed in such a way as to protect coppice and regeneration and where there is heavy grazing, the shrub layer is destroyed and any regrowth is eaten.

Effects of Grazing on the Ecology of Woodland

In a recent detailed study of the effects of grazing on the ecology of woodland, based on fieldwork in the New Forest, Putnam (1986) points out that the effects of grazing are not restricted to vegetational change and that '. . . through its dominating effect upon the vegetation, the intense grazing pressure has repercussions *throughout* the system . . . until it affects in practice the whole ecological shape and functioning of the New Forest system.'

The nature of the effects depends to a large extent on the density of stocking and the manipulation of the stocking density is consequently one of the most important ways of managing this type of woodland. Centuries of grazing tend to alter the ground flora with broadleaved herbs losing out to grasses and bryophytes (Pigott 1983). In some circumstances the alteration in the ground flora leads to a reduction in the number of species, in others, as with the grasslands of the New Forest, it can lead to the development of an interesting flora (Tubbs 1986). The changes in vegetation caused by grazing, in turn, affect the populations of invertebrates, birds and mammals. Indeed, the exclusion of grazing can sometimes initiate changes in the ground vegetation which will lead to the diminution or even extinction of certain species. In the upland woods, for example, species such as the coarse grasses, bilberry and

greater woodrush grow vigorously once released from grazing but they tend to smother smaller herbs and the carpets of bryophytes. Since many of these upland woods are important sites for Atlantic bryophytes, such losses could be significant (Ratcliffe 1968, Edwards 1986).

Effects of Grazing on Natural Regeneration

In areas where grazing has long been a practice, such as the New Forest, there is a complicated interrelationship between grazing and natural regeneration. In simple terms the main periods of tree regeneration take place when the grazing pressure is at its lowest (Peterken and Tubbs 1965, Morgan 1987). In the case of large areas of ancient

Grazing by sheep is very frequent in ancient woodlands of the uplands. This area at Maentwrog, Gwynedd, has been heavily grazed by sheep, and little ground vegetation remains

woodland, the long-term view might be that grazing will fluctuate, and even if grazing pressure is at present too high, in the future it will probably change and a new phase of regeneration will take place.

Where there is over-grazing of smaller areas of woodland, especially if, as in the upland grazed woods, the woods were not traditionally intensively grazed, the problem is more immediate. Although the trampling of grazing animals can expose new mineral surfaces which improve the rate of germination (Miles and Kinnaird 1979), if grazing continues unchecked the young seedlings will be regularly browsed and the wood will slowly thin out as trees die or are felled. The effect on the conservation value of a wood is especially bad where there is a high density of stock which does not feed from the vegetation within the wood, but is fed with hay or concentrates. When this happens, the ground flora of the wood is destroyed and the nutrient levels within the wood are artificially increased.

Management of Grazed Woodland
Control of Grazing
Where grazing is threatening the survival of ancient woodland, the remedy is either to:

1 exclude grazing;
2 reduce, but not exclude grazing;
3 fence off part of a wood at any time and to throw open the fenced areas once the new trees are tall enough.

In practice it is quite difficult to know which is the best course of action to take. If these woods are to be managed at all the stock needs to be fenced out for a decade or more, which is the time it takes for natural regeneration, or newly planted trees, to grow beyond the reach of the browsing animals. For nature conservation, the aim should be to regenerate a semi-natural wood with native trees and shrubs through natural regeneration.

The total exclusion of grazing is very difficult to enforce and is not always beneficial

in nature conservation terms. There is no doubt, however, that many ancient woods would benefit from a significant reduction in the amount of grazing. If there is to be a reduction in the number of animals grazing a wood, considerably greater control over grazing is required than is normal at present. In addition, careful monitoring is necessary to ensure that the effects of the reduction are beneficial to natural regeneration and the nature conservation value of the wood. It is possible to protect individual trees with tree shelters but this will not prevent the grazing and browsing of the other vegetation.

Encouragement of Natural Regeneration
If natural regeneration is to be successful, it may be necessary to do more than just fence off part of the wood in rotation. Many of the upland woods are dominated by oak and birch, at least on the drier more acid soils, and both these species require high levels of light for regeneration and benefit from some ground disturbance. If the canopy remains closed when the wood is fenced, rowan and holly will regenerate well, but the regeneration of oak and birch will be confined to margins and glades.

The alder woods on wet soils also require some canopy openings if regeneration of both alder and sallow is to be satisfactory. It is only the ash-wych elm stands on base-rich but not necessarily moist soils that will regenerate satisfactorily, if slowly, under closed stands. This is because elm, ash, lime, hazel and hawthorn are all capable of regeneration in the shade. If an upland oakwood can only be regenerated by felling some of the standing trees, and the oak stand is already closed, should regeneration be encouraged? The answer may be yes if the aim is to grow timber, but if it is to maintain an oakwood in the landscape it may be better to wait until the stand begins to break up naturally.

If the manager of the wood feels that he or she must do something to help regeneration, it is feasible to fell small patches of mature trees so that regeneration can take place in them. A simpler option is include some of the surrounding open land within the wood's ring fence. This will allow the spread by natural regeneration of species such as oak and birch and increase the structural diversity of the wood without the need to fell mature trees.

Fences, Walls and Hedges

The conservation value of woodland boundaries is discussed in Chapter 9. In grazed woods, the most common form of stock control is some form of wire fencing. Agate (1986) has written a most useful practical guide to fencing including sections on design and siting, materials and construction, and gates and stiles. Full details of the use of spring steel forest fences are available in a Forestry Commission leaflet (Pepper and Tee 1986). Another Forestry Commission leaflet describes the construction of badger gates (Rowe 1976). In many upland woods stone walls are the traditional form of stock control and an excellent guide to their construction, maintenance and repair is available (Brooks 1983). A similar guide is also available for the management of hedges (Brooks 1984).

Deer

There are probably well over a million deer in Britain. The number of deer has been increasing for a long time, partly because of the increase in areas of woodland over the past eighty years, and it is likely to continue increasing. The relationship between deer and the nature conservation value of woodland is a complicated one, and there is a need for more research on this subject. The Agriculture and Food Research Council has organised a research programme to consider the interrelationship between herbivores and their habitats, but results will not be available for a number of years. Even so, there is a considerable literature on deer and woodland management (Prior 1968, 1983, 1987; Chapman 1975; Rackham 1989; Watson 1983; Whitehead 1964). Further information on deer can be obtained from the British

The rabbit population is increasing, and in some areas it is so high that considerable damage is done to young coppice regrowth. The problem is serious at Scoska Wood in North Yorkshire, and rabbit fencing has been introduced. This is expensive, and it is especially difficult to make such fencing entirely rabbit-proof where the ground is rocky and uneven

Deer Society (Church Farm, Lower Basildon, Reading, Berkshire, RG8 9NH, 0734 844 094). This section discusses deer in the context of ancient woodland.

There are six main types of deer in Britain. As the different species do different kinds of damage, an understanding of their distribution is useful. The largest is the red deer which is mainly found in upland areas outside Wales, including Scotland, the Lake District and Devon and Cornwall. Red deer can also be found scattered locally throughout England.

The roe deer has a curious distribution. It is found throughout Scotland and northern England and in the southern counties of Devon, Somerset, Dorset, Hampshire, Sussex and East Anglia, but is not found in Wales or the West Midlands. The explanation of this distribution is that by the eighteenth century roe had become almost extinct in England but was then reintroduced in Dorset. The southern and eastern English roe are descended from this reintroduction.

The third most widely spread deer is the fallow. The present population is thought to have descended from introductions made by the Normans. Fallow are concentrated in southern and south-east England, but are also scattered locally throughout the country.

The populations of three further species, the sika (introduced from Japan in the late nineteenth century), which is found in the Highlands, the Lake District and parts of southern England; the Chinese water deer, which is now found in the East Midlands and Norfolk; and the muntjac (introduced from China), found in the Midlands, East Anglia and southern England, are also spreading.

Deer damage

There are a number of different kinds of deer damage. For young trees and recently cut coppice, the damage is most likely to take the form of browsing. This simply means that the deer are eating the leaves and shoots. The height of the browse line gives some indication of the types of deer causing the damage (see Table 9).

When assessing the height of the browse line, the possibility that heavy snow might have temporarily raised the ground level should be taken into account. Browsing by deer can often be distinguished from that of rabbits and hares by the shape of the cut end of the stem. With rabbits, the end of the cut stem is sharp and angled, with deer, it is rough and looks chewed.

The larger deer, such as the red, sika and fallow, tend to prefer grazing to browsing. The other main type of damage is done to the bark of trees. This can take two forms: first there is fraying, which is the damage that is caused by deer at certain times of the year by rubbing their antlers up and down the trunk in order to remove velvet; the second is bark stripping or peeling, which is caused by the deer pulling off bark with their teeth. When deer strip bark, they tend to leave behind vertical and parallel grooves in the tree caused by their teeth.

Table 9 The approximate maximum heights that deer will browse

muntjac	0.56m–0.86m (1ft 10in–2ft 10in)[*]
roe	1.2m (4ft)
fallow or sika	1.4m (4ft 6in)
red	1.5m (5ft)

[*]muntjac often browse to the second height by standing on their hind legs

(Source: R. Prior, 1983, p21)

Vulnerability of ancient woodland to deer damage

The problem with ancient woodland is that the best mode of management for nature conservation is also the best for deer conservation. A well-managed coppice, for example, will be made up of a matrix of small areas each having coppice of a different number of years growth. This is absolutely ideal habitat for roe and muntjac deer: there is plenty of easily obtainable browse; there is plenty of thick cover and the open areas are small enough for the deer to feel safe. Similarly, the small-scale management operations which are best for nature conservation in high forest areas make the woodland concerned especially suitable for deer.

Reducing deer damage in ancient woodland

The only way in the long term of reducing deer damage is to control the size of the deer population by culling. The larger the population the more likely it is that there will be deer damage. Shooting is the main form of deer control and to make this easier, it is important to have some wide rides or open areas so that it is possible to see the deer to be shot. Such open areas are also likely to be beneficial, if managed correctly, for general conservation (see Chapter 9). If the habitat is changed suddenly by clear felling, for example, deer are likely to leave a wood. Theoretically, therefore, if the whole of an ancient wood was coppiced at once, it would become very open and it is possible that the coppice would be able to grow above browsing height before the deer returned. The problem with this method, of course, is that the coppice would always be of the same age and it would not develop into a mosaic of different aged habitats.

There is a possibility that deer damage could be reduced if there was greater public access in woodland. This may be true in some circumstances but it is more likely that deer will simply learn to visit the wood when people are not about. In some cases, increased public access is thought to lead to an increase in bark stripping by deer because their normal feeding habits are disrupted (Prior 1983).

Deer fencing

Deer fencing is very expensive, never foolproof and is unlikely to last for more than ten or twelve years (Cooper and Mutch 1978). There is a considerable literature on deer fencing, and the subject is not dealt with in detail here (Agate 1986, Pepper and Tee 1986). In heavy snow, even the best deer fence is ineffective. In addition, deer leaps should be made so that deer who do manage to get inside the fence are able to get out. Electric fencing may be more suitable in protecting small areas typical of ancient woods. Fencing can also be used to protect small groups of trees and individual coppice stools.

Protection of individual trees

In some circumstances where, for example, standards are grown in coppice, or in areas of high forest, it may be necessary to protect individual trees from deer damage. Tree shelters will provide full protection for trees in their first season but they soon grow out of the top of the shelter. If the shelters are the standard 1.2m (4ft), they should provide adequate protection after the first season for muntjac and roe, but will not do so for fallow, sika or red deer. Further details on the protection of individual trees are given by Pepper, Rowe and Tee (1984).

Another way to protect individual trees is to make use of chemical deterrents (Pepper 1978). These are little used in this country but are popular on the Continent. Most are only suitable on dormant shoots and have to be painted or sprayed on to the leading shoot. This is time-consuming work but it is quite useful for dealing with small areas of standard trees. It is not feasible, however, for coppice because there are too many shoots to deal with.

Pollards
Treatment of Old Pollards

As pollarding generally ceased as a form of woodland management before the beginning of this century, there are now many old pollards with extremely large branches. These old pollards are often remarkably resilient and can live to a great age. There have, for example, been very few deaths over the last hundred years in the population of old oak pollards at Staverton Park in Suffolk. Sometimes, however, the very large branches make the tree unstable and in some species, such as willows, it is a common sight to see overgrown pollards whose branches are begining to fall

Pollarding enables the new shoots to grow out of the reach of grazing animals. At Castlemorton Common, near Malvern, Worcestershire, the vigorous regrowth of black poplar pollards after a season can be clearly seen. Other species which usually pollard well include willow, ash and lime

over and break off. If possible it is best to reintroduce pollarding before a tree reaches the point of collapse. A full review of recent experience in the re-pollarding of large neglected pollards has been produced by Mitchell (1989).

Pollarding

Traditionally, pollarding would take place when the branches were no more than ten or twenty years old and the process would have been quite simple. The situation is different with today's overgrown pollards, where the branches can have reached a very large size indeed. It is dangerous to use chain-saws for pollarding, and if they have to be used only experienced and well-trained individuals should undertake the task. Overgrown willow pollards are particularly dangerous to cut. It is safer, though still quite a tricky operation, to use a bow saw. With large, old pollards it is easiest to saw through the poles from a position at the top of the bole or trunk of the tree. In the past, pollarding will often have taken place in the summer because the foliage was used as fodder. For the purposes of nature conservation autumn or winter pollarding is more suitable.

Survival of Pollarded Trees

Pollarding has been reintroduced on a small scale compared to coppicing and there is consequently less evidence on the rates of survival. Its success will depend, to some extent, on the species concerned. Some trees, such as willow, ash and lime are most unlikely to die as a result of pollarding, while with others such as beech, there is very likely to be failure. Pollarding of hornbeams is generally successful (97 per cent of 59 trees in Epping

The first of this pair of photographs shows a group of hornbeams early in the season following pollarding. Some of the poles have been sawn up and stacked. One or two of the trees are beginning to sprout. The second photograph was taken later on in the same season. All the trees are now showing vigorous growth

Forest). The response of oak is variable. At Killerton in Devon, six out of seven old oaks were successfully re-pollarded and in Epping Forest most of the re-pollarded oaks have survived but at Hatfield Forest, Essex, nine out of ten re-pollarded oaks died.

Pollards and Danger

Many overgrown pollards are inherently unstable because of their growth form. In addition, many areas of old pasture woodland, especially those found in the old royal forests, parks and woodland commons have a long tradition of public access. Where there is access, and the pollards are considered dangerous, the responsible landowner may have to pollard the trees in the interests of public safety, even though in conservation terms there will be a loss of habitat (Griffin and Watkins 1986).

New Pollards

Where old pollards already exist it is good nature conservation practice to form new pollards. This maintains the traditional form of tree management in the area and means that when the old pollards eventually die, there will be suitable habitats for the species which pollards support. The new pollarded individuals should be of the same species as those already in existence. In general terms, the shorter the bole, the easier it is to pollard a tree. However, there is no point in pollarding a tree below the browsing level of the animals which graze the area concerned.

To be safe, it is best to make the first cut at 2.5–3m (8ft 2in–9ft 10in) from ground level. In general, the first cutting should be made when the stem of the tree is about 150mm (6in) in diameter. Pollarding can be instigated on larger trees but the initial felling is then more difficult. The establishment of new pollards could be particularly useful in areas of wood pasture where there is public access as it would show visitors how the older pollards came into being.

Pollards and Continuity of Habitat

When pollarding is reintroduced in an area

with a number of old pollards, it is important that only a proportion is cut in any one season and that the trees pollarded should be scattered over the area concerned. This will help the survival and spread of rare species. Where the pollard is growing by itself, the remaining pollard bole becomes a very important habitat and any cut branches should be allowed to rot nearby so that species living on them have a chance of spreading to the bole.

Conservation of Species Living on Pollards

A number of epiphytic species seem to be unable to colonise new sites, although they are able to survive where they already exist. Some are very rare. One species, *Lobaria scrobiculata*, for example, is thought to grow only on seventy-two trees south of the Scottish Highlands (Harding and Rose,

1986). Some beetles associated with wood pasture are also very rare. At Moccas Park in Herefordshire there is the only known breeding population of *Hypebaeus flavipes* and this is found on a small number of oak pollards but not on surrounding old standard oaks.

In these circumstances, it is very important to ensure that old individual pollards are not removed or damaged. The owner can do a lot to help conserve these trees by making sure that chemical sprays do not drift over from nearby agricultural land, that visitors do not take away dead wood and that any younger trees do not totally overtop the old pollards.

Other problems owners can do very little about: these include the incidence of air pollution which is considered to be having an increasing effect on epiphyte communities in the south and east and the lowering of water tables.

Management Guidelines

- The general aim should be the establishment of a balance between grazing and regeneration
- Where grazing is threatening the survival of a wood, or reducing its conservation value, it should be reduced
- Grazing and browsing animals should not be totally excluded from ancient woods, as they are an element of natural woodland
- In addition to the control of grazing, it may be necessary to open up the canopy of some woods to encourage the regeneration of oak and birch
- If possible the woodland fence should be extended to include some peripheral areas where natural regeneration can take advantage of the lack of shade

- The deer population should be controlled by culling
- Tree shelters can be used to protect individual trees from deer damage in their first season
- Overgrown pollards should be repollarded before they reach the point of collapse but only if there is good evidence that they will continue to grow
- Where there is a group of old pollards, pollarding should be reintroduced over a number of years in order to maintain continuity of habitat
- New young pollards should be made

In many areas, old parkland has been ploughed up and converted to arable land. Here at Windsor Forest, the old pollard oaks stand in a recently cultivated area. In such cases, great care should be taken to prevent cultivation of the ground too near to the trees, and to stop spray drift and fire damage

9 Habitats Associated with Ancient Woodland

The original natural woodland would not have been a continuous area covered with dense trees. There would have been many different glades and clearings of assorted shapes and sizes caused by falling trees, grazing animals, fire and particular types of soil condition. There would also have been areas of bog and heath, outcrops of rock and cliffs, ponds and rivers. In semi-natural ancient woodland today, some similar clearings and open areas have been created naturally but the vast majority are the result of human activity. Frequently found examples include woodland rides and paths, ponds dug to provide water in case of fire and areas managed for game conservation. This chapter deals with the management of such habitats for nature conservation.

Value of Associated Habitats for Conservation

These associated habitats increase the overall diversity of woodland by encouraging the growth of species which make use of both the closed canopy of woodland and the more open habitat. Other species which are characteristic of that particular habitat and are more or less independent of the woodland can also survive. Indeed, in some parts of the country, and especially eastern England, the best example of a particular associated habitat may be found within woodland as equivalent habitat outside woodland has been destroyed. Woodland rides, for example, may be the best unimproved grassland in an area; the only natural ponds and stream channels in an area may be those in ancient woods; butterflies which used to be supported by

meadows long since ploughed up can now survive on the tall herb communities which grow along the edges of rides (Warren and Fuller, in press).

Often these areas are not part of the productive woodland area and managing them in a way sympathetic for wildlife does not cause any significant loss of woodland income. Moreover, there may be benefits to the forester: wide open rides are usually the best for butterflies but they are also drier and hence form better extraction routes. Programmes of ride widening and mowing carried out to improve pheasant shoots can benefit both plants and invertebrates (Robertson, Woodburn and Hill 1988).

Management of Associated Habitat

The amount of management required in the different types of non-woodland habitat varies enormously and they need to be considered separately. With some types of habitat, non-intervention is the best approach. This is true of screes, gorges and most other rock habitats and some wet, boggy areas. Clearings, on the other hand should usually be kept open by active management if necessary. Standing water bodies such as ponds are best managed to maintain at least part of their margins open and sunny – ponds which are wholly shaded and full of leaves attract few species. With streams and rivers it is best, again, to manage for a mixture of shaded and open sections.

The Woodland Edge
Conservation Value

The woodland edge, if managed correctly,

can form a useful transitional habitat between the woodland and the surrounding more open ground. It can be as important as the edges of internal rides and, like them, provides a variety of different types of habitat depending on orientation and management (Ellenberg 1988). When a wood has a long, sinuous boundary, as is often the case with ancient woods, the edge habitat can cover a surprising amount of ground.

Apart from its inherent value for nature conservation, the boundary of a wood often needs to be managed as a stockproof barrier in the form of a hedge, fence or wall. The wood edge is usually the most visible part of a wood and, if managed well, it will help to show the public that the wood has been taken in hand. Well-managed wood edges will also help to ensure good relations with neighbouring landowners who are otherwise likely to be annoyed by the low overhanging

This woodland hedge at Bernwood Forest, Oxfordshire, contains a lot of blackthorn. This provides excellent habitat for the black hairstreak butterfly. Blackthorn has a tendency to grow suckers and invade surrounding agricultural land, and so needs to be regularly cut back

branches resulting from woodland neglect. Where a wood adjoins a public road, the edge needs to be managed carefully so that overhanging branches do not reduce visibility for passing traffic. It should also be borne in mind that the shade cast by trees can increase the likelihood of icy patches forming on roads adjoining woodland.

Ownership

Before starting to manage the woodland edge the ownership boundary should be determined accurately. If this is not done it can lead to difficulties with neighbouring owners. The normal rule is that where there is a bank and a ditch, both belong to the owner of the bank. Where there is a wood bank, therefore, the woodland owner also usually owns the ditch on the outside of the bank. Exceptions to this general rule may occur where a woodland owner has sold an adjoining field, and included the wood hedge in the sale so as to avoid the responsibility of managing it in the future.

In many cases there is no discernible bank or ditch. This may be because there never was a bank, or the bank has been destroyed when part of the wood was grubbed, or because the wood has spread over the years leaving the old boundary banks as historical features inside the wood. In cases like this the correct determination of the boundary may require close attention to the deeds.

Wood Banks

Wood banks are of great interest to archaeologists and to those interested in the history of particular sites. Because they are raised above the level of the surrounding land, they often contain species not found in the interior of the wood. Such features should not be disturbed when carrying out woodland management operations. Where a wood bank immediately adjoins a pasture field, stock should not be allowed to gain access to the bank as otherwise they will soon erode it by trampling. Care should be taken to avoid damage to the banks when cleaning out ditches adjoining ancient wood banks.

Management of Wood Hedges

The hedges around woods are often in a poor condition especially if the wood has been neglected. It is good nature conservation practice to restore the hedge, even if the wood is surrounded by arable land and the hedge is not required as a stockproof barrier. The hedge habitat adds diversity to the wood. Properly maintained hedges are also an efficient means of sheltering the interior of the wood and can help to reduce the spread of agricultural spray drift into the wood.

Hedge history and management has been covered by Pollard, Hooper and Moore (1974) and Muir and Muir (1987). Generally wood hedges should be managed as other hedges but there are a few differences. There is no point, for example, in managing the hedge by layering or coppicing if it is overshadowed by woodland trees and overgrown coppice. If the hedges are to be restored this should be done at the same time as coppicing is carried out in the section of the wood adjoining the hedge. This ensures that conditions are suitable for the new hedge growth to survive. Whether a hedge should be layered or coppiced depends on the locally traditional practice of hedge management and the current state of the hedge. If the wood adjoins grazed land, stock should be kept away from the hedge until it has become established.

One way of increasing the interest of a wood edge, and also of ensuring that wood hedges can grow well, is to coppice a narrow strip of woodland around the edge of the wood on a fairly short rotation. At Treswell Wood (Nottinghamshire), for example, a strip 3m (9ft 10in) wide has been coppiced all the way around the wood. This improves the overall woodland diversity by increasing the area of transitional woodland.

Other Boundary Features

Some old fences, fence posts, gates and so forth provide useful dead-wood habitat and can be of historical interest. This is certainly true, for example, of the few remaining old park pales and of the old wooden gates, which show considerable regional variation in construction and design but which are now becoming quite rare.

Wire fences are admittedly of rather less interest, although some of the early forms of barbed wire from the last century are collected by enthusiasts. In stone-wall country, many of the walls around woods are thought largely to date from parliamentary enclosure and to be 150–200 years old at most. Recent archaeological work, however, suggests that some walls are of considerable age (Wildgoose 1987). In terms of nature conservation, the main value of walls lies in stock control, although they do provide additional dry-stone habitat for mosses, plants, some insects, small mammals and birds.

Rides and Ride Management

The patterns of rides found in ancient woods have arisen in different ways and at different times. Some ride systems are of medieval or even earlier origin, some have complicated geometric rides (laid out in the eighteenth century), others have concrete surface rides dating from World War II. Ride systems can therefore be of considerable historical and cultural interest and should be conserved for that reason. In addition, the vegetation of rides may have developed over a number of centuries and it is important to continue or restore management of the rides in order to conserve the species living in the habitat and the seed bank.

Rides vary widely in type of construction, age, and conservation value. The type of least value for nature conservation are metalled rides or those built of concrete. The hard surfaces of these rides have little conservation value and this type of ride should be kept to a minimum. It may, however, be better to accept the construction of some rides of this sort in order to enable the wood to be managed economically and to reduce the damage to other rides when extracting timber in wet weather. Even these rides commonly have a narrow strip of vegetation growing between the wheel tracks, and can also have valuable ride edges. The concrete itself is sometimes colonised by plants such as stonecrop, and may be used as a basking site by lizards and snakes.

Making New Rides

Wherever possible, use should be made of the existing rides but, in some circumstances, it may be necessary to make new ones. If a wood is under more than one ownership, or part of a wood has been grubbed up, for example, the existing ride pattern may not allow sufficient access to all parts of the wood. In other cases, the current rides may not be suitable for modern machinery. If new ones are made, account should be taken of the need to maintain rides in the future, and whether enough funds and labour are likely to be available.

Another reason for making new rides is to increase the proportion of ride habitat or to provide additional links between rides and clearings so as to allow for the migration of species. In addition, the exposed mineral soil may be a suitable substrate or nutrient medium for the germination of woodland plants. Moreover, in limestone areas where there is no need to introduce surface material, new rides may make good new habitat. If new rides are going to be made, great care should be taken not to damage any woodland habitat of particular conservation interest.

Materials Used in Ride Maintenance

In clay areas hardcore may be needed to keep rides passable in the winter, especially if the removal of timber or coppice poles is being considered or there is much public access to the woodland. The type of hardcore used can have an effect on the ride vegetation. The use of limestone rubble, or old bricks with lime mortar could, for example, change the pH level significantly. In addition, new species could be introduced to a wood by the use of rubble which included some weed seeds. Where public access is important, wood chips or shredded bark are possible substitutes for hardcore. Another way of making rides passable is to fill the ruts with faggots of wood.

The Ideal Ride for Conservation

There are no hard-and-fast rules as to how rides should be managed, and standard ride management plans should not be applied to woods all over the country. In general, ride management should result in a gradation from short grass in the middle, through taller grass and herbs on the outside of the ride, to a shrubby border to the woodland proper. When establishing this gradation the full width of the ride should be maintained.

(Above) *Although this ride in Math and Elsea Woods, Kesteven, Lincolnshire is less overgrown than that shown in the lower photograph opposite, widening it would be beneficial for the plants growing in it and for butterflies and other insects. It is often difficult to judge how wide to make a ride when the leaves are off the trees in the winter. The ride in this photograph would be almost entirely shaded in the summer*

(Opposite, above) *In this part of Bernwood Forest, Oxfordshire, the ancient woodland has been replanted with conifers, which can be seen growing on both sides of the ride. Wide rides like this have many benefits for*

nature conservation. The openness makes them a distinct habitat within the woodland, and they can support a wide range of insects and plants

(Opposite, below) *This ride in Bowd Lane Wood, Northamptonshire, is almost totally overgrown by woody shrubs. The dense shade cast by this growth means that very few plants grow in the ride. The narrowness of the ride forces everyone walking along it on to the same thin strip of ground, making it very compacted. Rides such as this are almost impassable, and of little value for nature conservation. The vegetation should be cut back so the ride is at least 10m (33ft) wide*

Rides of a sinuous shape and rides with un-even edges will have a greater proportion of ride edge habitat than straight rides.

Width

Where the edges of rides are marked by ditches, there is little difficulty in knowing how wide the ride has been in the past. If a wood has been neglected, the rides have usually been encroached by woody vegetation, and sometimes quite large trees. These trees and shrubs need to be cleared back to the ditch if any attempt is going to be made to try to restore the ride vegetation. If there is no ditch to work to, then the open rides should be made at least 10m (33ft) wide, and preferably wider.

Rides and Shade

It is the openness of rides which makes them a distinct habitat from the woodland itself. If they become too shady they lose a lot of intrinsic interest and there will be a substantial decline in the number of plants and insects they support. Many invertebrates have annual life cycles with the result that whole populations can be eliminated if conditions are unfavourable for just a few years. Shady rides also tend to get very wet and take a long time to dry out making them difficult to use for extraction purposes. In general, therefore, rides should be kept open (Warren and Fuller, in press).

Ride orientation is important because in general terms those rides which receive most sunlight make the best habitat. The south-facing edges of rides running from west to east are especially important. The orientation is of little importance, however, if trees over-hang the ride or are so tall that they prevent the sun reaching the floor of the ride. If the ride is orientated so that the prevailing wind blows along it, this will have the effect of making the ride very cold for butterflies and game. The wind can be reduced by allowing the ride to curve to one side at the edge of the wood so that there is a narrow screen of trees sheltering the ride.

As much conservation coppicing is done on a longer rotation than traditional coppicing, even where coppicing has been reintroduced, rides are likely to be shaded by coppice growth for a considerably longer period than in the past. One way around this problem is to have narrow strips of coppice adjoining the rides on a shorter rotation than the rest of the wood.

Cutting Ride Vegetation

The central section of the rides should be mown infrequently. Grass cuttings should be removed otherwise there will be a build-up of nutrients which will attract the coarser vegetation. Areas of rush and bramble will need regular cutting if a grassy sward is desired. At Kirton Wood in Nottinghamshire, a roller has been successfully used to control the growth of coarse vegetation. The timing of ride cutting is important especially for the taller growth along the edges. Herbaceous vegetation should be cut in August or September after the plants have seeded.

The tall woody growth along the edges of the ride should be cut in late winter. The shrubs found along ride edges, such as sallow, alder buckthorn, hawthorn, blackthorn and spindle are valuable food plants. If the purple emperor butterfly is found in the area, sallow should be allowed to grow along ride edges and this should be coppiced to provide adequate food for the butterfly's larvae (Willmott 1987).

Cutting along ride edges should be done only every other year and only one side at a time, or with alternate lengths cut each year. This ensures that there is always a supply of tall herbs and grasses able to flower fully, and so provide food for many adult insects. The

This pair of photographs shows ride management in part of Bentley Woods, Wiltshire. The woodland itself has been replanted with broadleaves and conifers. The first photograph shows a narrow, metalled ride which will remain shaded for much of the day. The second photograph shows wide verges which are beneficial for an extensive range of insects and plants

shrubby edges should be cut less frequently, perhaps once every five to ten years. A more detailed discussion of ride management is provided by Warren and Fuller (in press).

Wet Patches in Rides
Wet areas within rides should be maintained wherever possible as they add to the ecological diversity of the wood. They are often associated with shady rides where the sun is not able to dry out the ride. Ideally, important rides should not be used by heavy machinery in very wet conditions. If this is inevitable, from time to time, it is necessary to judge whether drainage or the occasional churning up of the ground has the lesser long-term effect for nature conservation. Old ruts with temporary puddles can themselves add interesting habitat diversity to a ride.

Glades, Clearings, Firebreaks and Deer Lawns
Origin of Open Areas
An immense range of different kinds of clearings and open areas can be found in ancient woods. Some, such as the small openings caused by the death of a large tree or the failure of a small group of planted trees or coppice stools, are of a temporary nature. They eventually become overshadowed by the growth of adjoining trees. Even quite extensive open areas caused, for example, by exceptionally strong winds soon grow up as long as there is not too much grazing.

Other areas remain open for long periods of time. Most of these openings are kept open by specific management, as in the case of wide

Wherever possible care should be taken to avoid damaging rides when extracting wood and timber from ancient woodland. Sometimes, damage is inevitable however, and it is then often surprising how quickly the vegetation recovers. The two photographs are of the same ride in Leigh Woods, Avon, but taken a few years apart. The first shows the deep ruts in the ride caused by heavy equipment used to remove timber. The second shows the same ride after a few years' growth

Glades increase the ecological diversity of ancient woodland. When linked to rides they increase the length of shrubby ride-edge in a wood. Here at Monks Wood, Cambridgeshire, uneven-shaped glades have been cut adjoining one of the main rides

Such glades support distinct groups of invertebrates and allow birds such as sparrow hawks and owls to hunt within the wood. The sunny conditions increase the amount of nectar available for butterflies and other insects.

shooting rides, fire breaks and the areas under power lines, or by grazing, as in the case of deer lawns. Some, however, such as areas of dense bracken growth, can exist for many years with no direct management.

Conservation Value

Open areas increase the ecological diversity of an area of woodland. Small clearings, for example, allow the herb layer to grow more luxuriantly for a few years but most of the species will be the same as in the surrounding woodland. Larger and more permanent clearings tend to have their own distinct communities which may be grassland, heath or bog depending on the local conditions.

Occurrence of Open Areas

Many woods, especially in lowland Britain, have very few open areas and some have none at all. This is especially true of neglected coppice woodlands where the lack of management has resulted in a continuous canopy. Indeed, without specific management, open areas will only survive if there are very wet areas or stands of dense bracken, or if there is heavy grazing pressure.

Open areas are much more likely to be found in upland woods, especially if they are grazed. Lack of regeneration may itself be a nature conservation problem in woods with a sparse tree canopy (see Chapter 8).

(Above) *The junction of rides is often a convenient point to make a glade. This photograph shows a ride intersection in Bernwood Forest, Oxfordshire, where the trees have been cut back to form an open area which is beneficial to insects and plants*

(Opposite) *Streams and ponds in woods are usually very valuable habitats. In western and upland Britain, the high humidity in the areas adjoining streams makes them important sites for mosses and liverworts. There is plenty of dead wood in this stream at Hareshaw Dean, Northumberland. Such wood is an additional valuable habitat which should be retained where possible*

Management

Some form of mowing is often required to keep areas open. To stop trees encroaching on wet areas, it is sometimes possible to increase the wetness of the area by blocking exit drains. If cutting of the clearings is necessary similar principles as those for ride maintenance should be followed. The spread of bracken and bramble into open areas should be controlled by regular cutting or in exceptional circumstances by chemical means (see Chapter 4).

Some operations, such as the use of herbicides to maintain firebreaks and the fertilising and reseeding of deer lawns, are particularly deleterious to the nature conservation interest of these areas and should not be used in ancient woodland. Similar practices have eliminated many of the species from the surrounding fields. If a piece of herb-rich grassland, or perhaps an old green lane, is found adjoining a wood, it may be worth managing it with the wood in order to preserve its nature conservation interest.

Making New Open Areas

If a wood has few open areas, glades can be made to increase its ecological diversity. An obvious site would be the junction of some rides: this would be much easier to manage than an isolated site and would also allow the spread of species already growing in the rides. An alternative is to make a number of small glades along the side of a ride. There may be historical evidence – such as old maps – that glades or small fields used to exist in a wood, if so, these open areas could be restored. Make sure that the areas where glades are to be made do not contain woodland species which are of greater nature conservation interest than those likely to grow in the glade.

Areas of Water and Wet Areas

Streams, ponds and seepage zones in woods are very valuable habitats, and areas around them are often particularly rich in both woodland and non-woodland species. Springs within woods may be less contaminated with agricultural chemicals than elsewhere. Woodland streams may follow their natural meandering courses, and in western Britain the high humidity associated with streams has allowed many rare and unusual mosses and liverworts to survive. Ponds and areas of bog within woods can be scientifically important as sites which might contain deposits suitable for pollen analysis. They are also important habitat for frogs, newts, toads and grass snakes. Dead wood which has fallen into ponds provides additional habitat and should be retained.

Origin of Ponds

Ponds and pools in woods may be in the natural depressions left after the last ice age. Others have been deepened or dug to extract clay, gravel or some other mineral, to provide the power for machinery such as trip hammers or to provide a supply of water for horses and other draught animals (Rackham 1986a).

Creation of Ponds

If there are no ponds within a wood it may be desirable to make some by excavation or damming a stream. Great care should be taken that the area chosen for a pond is not one that is of greater value as a piece of wet ground. Natural watercourses should not be interfered with just to make a pond. If a stream is to be dammed, permission must be sought from the relevant water authority.

Management of Vegetation Around Ponds

Ponds should not be allowed to be completely shaded. The area to the south of the pond should generally be kept clear of trees and shrubs by regular coppicing or the making of a glade. Trees can be allowed to grow to the edge of the water on the northern edge. The only situation where growth of trees along the southern edge of a pond can be recommended is when a pond is rich in nutrients. In this case, shading by trees could reduce the amount of algal growth.

Drainage of Wet Areas

Some ancient woods have been drained by ditches in the past but the degree of drainage is usually less than in surrounding areas. Often, indeed, the reason a wood has survived is its situation on land which was difficult to drain. Ancient woods on wet sites may create management problems but they should be left undrained to conserve the characteristic animals and plants.

In some woods, such as Chalkney Wood in Essex, the vegetation of the small wet areas may be one of the most interesting and valuable habitats within the wood. Special care should be taken to resist the casual digging of ditches which could easily destroy this habitat without even noticeably improving the growing conditions in the rest of the wood.

Wet Areas and Woodland Management

The size of any fellings on wet ground should be considered carefully because the water table often rises once the trees are felled making it difficult to re-establish a crop. In wet woods particular care is needed to avoid the churning up of the ground during extraction of timber and very wet boggy ground may be best left as a non-productive area.

Maintenance of Ditches

In some instances, it may be necessary to dig ditches along rides to keep them dry, although even temporary puddles can have ecological interest. It will also be necessary to maintain any ditches on the wood's boundary. Ditches should be cleaned out in rotation, rather than all at once, as this will allow for greater continuity of the associated flora and fauna. Such maintenance is likely to expose new mineral surfaces and these can be beneficial for the germination of plants such as primroses and broad-leaved helleborines.

Rocks, Screes, Quarries, Limestone Pavements

Conservation Value of Rock Outcrops

It is difficult to generalise about the value of rock outcrops for conservation as they vary

At Cringlebarrow in Lancashire, yew and birch trees grow in areas of limestone pavement. The deep cracks known as grykes in such pavements can provide habitat for a wide range of species

so much. Cliff ledges and gorges in western Britain are often the only ungrazed parts of woods and hence the only areas to develop rich tall-herb communities. Extensive moss mats may develop on the thin soils or bare rock and in sheltered, humid conditions, these areas can support rare species. The dry and sunny conditions associated with screes and rock outcrops support a very different group of species. The deep cracks known as grykes in limestone pavements can harbour a wide range of species which are not found in the surrounding countryside.

A number of ancient woods containing steep cliffs, such as Lady Park Wood in Gloucestershire, Downton Gorge in Herefordshire and Lathkill Dale in Derbyshire, are so important for conservation that they have been designated National Nature Reserves. Some of Britain's rarest trees, a group of endemic whitebeams, grow on outcrops of limestone in south-west England, South Wales and Arran.

In heavily grazed woodland, steep cliffs and rock outcrops may be the only places where sheep are unable to go and are hence the only places where natural regeneration of tree species is able to take place. Rock outcrops are, therefore, of great importance in some of the upland ancient woods and these areas should not be planted up with trees but be seen as possible sites for natural regeneration.

Management of Woodland Growing on Rock Outcrops

Most types of rock habitat are of little interest to foresters because of the difficulty of managing trees that are growing on them. In general, rock habitats should be left undisturbed. Planting among the rocks may prove to be more expensive than allowing natural regeneration to take place and harvesting costs can be very high with this sort of site. Limestone pavements and related limestone screes are of national importance. In the past they have been removed for garden stone but special measures may now be taken to protect

The limestone gorge at Downton in Herefordshire has been designated a National Nature Reserve. The ancient woodland along the gorge along the River Teme contains many old lime trees. Many of the paths built in the late-eighteenth century by the owner of Downton Estate, Richard Payne Knight, to view the picturesque gorge have now disappeared

The designation of a wood as a National Nature Reserve does not necessarily protect it from rubbish dumping. This assortment of household waste was found at Glen Nant in Argyll

them under the Wildlife and Countryside Act 1981.

Rubbish and Litter
Rubbish and Nature Conservation

Woods are often used as dumping grounds for a variety of different kinds of rubbish. The effects of this activity on the conservation value of the woodland concerned depends on the type of rubbish though, in practice, the scenery is more likely to be affected than the wildlife. Small amounts of paper litter and the odd tin can or bottle look unsightly and may be an encouragement for other more extensive dumping. In themselves, however, they have little long-term effect on the habitat except that some small mammals may be trapped in bottles and containers which have held oil or chemicals are potentially damaging to the immediate surroundings.

Large amounts of paper litter, old tyres, tin cans and plastic and larger fragments of machinery and old cars destroy the ground vegetation on which they are dumped. The rubbish itself, however, may be used by hibernating animals. A potentially more serious form of dumping is that of soil, garden waste, hay bales, agricultural waste such as old potatoes or sugar beet, hardcore and other rubble. This type of dumping is likely to alter the vegetation of the areas on which they are dumped and may introduce potentially aggressive weedy species.

Management Guidelines

- Habitats associated with ancient woodland should be managed to sustain and increase the woodland's ecological diversity
- The woodland edge should be managed to provide transitional habitat between the wood and the surrounding habitat
- If grazing is not part of the management regime of the wood, and there is adjoining pasture, a stockproof hedge or fence should be maintained
- Wood banks should be preserved
- The established ride system should be maintained
- The management of rides should result in a variety of ride types, some being wide and sunny, others being narrow and shady
- Most of the herbaceous ride vegetation should be cut in late August or September to allow time for seeds to ripen
- Narrow strips of coppice should be cut along both sides of any wide 'open' rides
- Glades in ungrazed woods should be kept open by regularly cutting the vegetation

- New small glades can be made as long as the area cleared has no inherent special conservation value
- Avoid disturbing woodland ponds, streams and bogs during normal management operations
- If new ponds are made make sure that the new habitat is of more value than the one it replaces
- In large woods ensure that some ponds are shaded and some open
- Avoid disturbing cliffs, screes, limestone pavements and other rock habitats
- Do not fell trees in gorges or on screes
- Do not shade out limestone pavement areas by planting
- Stop the dumping of rubbish in ancient woodland

Herbicides

A range of herbicides is available and it is often difficult to decide which is the best for a particular site. This appendix provides information about the five herbicides which are most likely to be of use in ancient woodland (see Chapter 4). They have all been used in National Nature Reserves. The following accounts are based on the work of Marrs and Griffith (1986) in A. S. Cooke (ed) *The Use of Herbicides in Nature Reserves*. Forestry may require the use of other herbicides: some of the herbicides used regularly by the Forestry Commission such as propyzamide (Kerb) are unlikely to cause unwanted side-effects (Sale, Tabbush and Lane 1986).

Ammonium Sulphamate (Amcide)

This is most likely to be used to kill unwanted woody species such as rhododendron and sycamore and is effective when applied to the cut stumps of both these species. It is not a selective herbicide and kills most plants. It has a low toxicity to mammals and birds but is harmful to fish; it is unlikely to have toxic effects in the soil after two months.

Ammonium sulphamate can be applied in solution or in the form of crystals. If crystals are used, it is relatively easy to avoid damage to vegetation growing around the plants which are to be killed. It is important that the crystals are applied to the surface of the cut as soon as possible after it has been made, and certainly on the same day. The stumps should have 'V'-shaped notches cut into them as this helps to keep the crystals in place. About 15g of the crystals should be applied for each 25mm of stem diameter that has been cut.

For very dense areas of rhododendron, it may be too time-consuming to use crystals. If spray is used, it should be used at a concentration of 400g/litre, and applied to the cut stumps or regrowth 1.2m or less tall. The stumps and stems should be completely covered with the solution and, if possible, a wetting agent should be added to the solution. Sometimes a second application is necessary. To prevent the herbicide from getting washed off the target plants, ammonium sulphamate should not be used, whether in crystal or liquid form, on wet days or when rain is expected.

Asulam (Asulox)

This is a systemic herbicide which is most likely to be used in ancient woodland for the control of bracken. It will also kill certain grasses and is particularly harmful to ferns and docks. It has a low toxicity for animals and does not persist for long in the soil. Bracken should be sprayed between mid-July and early August, when the fronds are completely unfurled, but before they harden off.

The effects of the application of asulam will not be apparent until the following season when over 90 per cent of the fronds should be killed. If there is no change of management such as the introduction of mowing, however, the bracken is likely to reinvade the treated area within five years. The treated area should not be grazed or mown within a week of spraying: 4.4kg of the active ingredient is needed to kill 1ha (2½ acres) of bracken. It should be applied with a standard knapsack sprayer at a rate of between 100 and 500 litres/ha. The solution can be applied more efficiently if a wetting agent is used.

Fosamine Ammonium (Krenite)

This is a selective herbicide which can be used to kill most woody species, although some such as rhododendron are resistant. It does not normally affect most herbaceous plants or grasses, and it has a low toxicity to animals. It is not thought to damage soil bacteria or soil fungi and because it degrades rapidly, it is safe to use near watercourses.

If used as a spray, it has to be applied to all the foliage, and hence for trees and shrubs over 2m in height it is easier to cut them down first and apply the herbicide to the regrowth. Because it is a non-systemic herbicide, fosamine can be used to kill parts of a tree while leaving the rest of the tree alive. It should be applied at the rate of 2.9–4.8kg of the active ingredient per ha (2½ acres). The best months to apply fosamine are August and September; the leaves will not fall prematurely, but buds should not develop in the spring.

Glyphosate (Roundup)

Glyphosate can be used to kill the stumps of unwanted woody species. It is a non-selective herbicide which kills most plants and therefore great care should be taken that spray does not drift onto areas that are not being treated. Because of its broad spectrum of activity, glyphosate should not be used for bracken control in ancient woodland: asulam should be used instead. It has a low toxicity to animals and should not persist for long in the soil although there is evidence that in some circumstances it can persist for longer than the other herbicides discussed here.

The timing of application is very important. If it is being sprayed onto leaves, glyphosate should be applied when the leaves are still actively growing. If stumps of deciduous trees or shrubs are being painted with glyphosate, they may be killed with solutions with a concentration as low as 1.8–3.6 per cent of active ingredient.

Wetting agents should not be used because they can reduce the effectiveness of the herbicide and even render it useless. One way of increasing the efficiency of glyphosate, however, is to add 'Mixture B' as 2 per cent of the spray volume (Clipsham 1984, Tabbush 1987). This additive not only increases the rate and amount of uptake of the herbicide, but it also shortens the time which must be allowed before rain from twenty-four hours to ten hours.

Triclopyr (Garlon)

This herbicide can be used to kill most woody plants and can be used in ancient woodland to get rid of invasive species. It can kill many broadleaved plants but has little effect on grasses. Triclopyr has a low toxicity to animals but formulations can be dangerous to fish and should therefore be kept away from watercourses. It degrades rapidly in the soil.

In ancient woods it is probably best applied to cut stumps, but it can also be applied as a foliar spray and as a winter shoot spray. The whole of the stump including cut surfaces and bark should be painted immediately after the trees or shrubs have been felled. They should be painted with a solution of 24g of active ingredient per litre of diesel or 48g per litre of water. Triclopyr is effective when applied in any season but should not be used in very hot weather or when rain is expected within two hours.

Bibliography

Adams, I. H. *Descriptive List of Plans in the Scottish Record Office* (HMSO, three volumes: 1966, 1970, 1974)

Adams, I. H. and Timperley, L. R. *Descriptive List of Plans in the Scottish Record Office* (Volume 4) (Scottish Record Office, 1988)

Agate, E. *Fencing* (BTCV, 1986)

Alcock, N. *Old Title Deeds* (Phillimore, 1986)

Amphlett, J. 'Botany', in *The Victoria History of the County of Worcester* (Constable, 1901)

Anderson, M. L. *A History of Scottish Forestry* (Nelson, 1967)

Armstrong, L. *Woodcolliers and Charcoal Burning* (Coach Publishing House, 1978)

Babb, L. M. C. 'Bark peeling and tanning in the Forest of Wyre', *Folklife* (**18**, 1980) 49–53

Bain, C. *Native Pinewoods in Scotland: A Review 1957–1987* (RSPB, 1987)

Ball, D. F. and Stevens, P. A. 'The role of ancient woodlands in conserving undisturbed soils in Britain', *Biological Conservation* (**19**, 1981) 163–76

Barton, P. R. 'Woodland management in the late seventeenth century', *Hertfordshire Archaeology* (**7**, 1979) 181–200

Beaver, S. H. 'Forests in the north-west Midlands of England', *Forestry* (**47**, 1974) 129–44

Beckett, K. and Beckett, G. *Planting Native Trees and Shrubs* (Jarrold, 1979)

Beevor, H. 'Norfolk Woodlands, from the evidence of contemporary chronicles', *Quarterly Journal of Forestry* (**19**, 1925) 87–110

Begley, C. D. and Coates, A. E. 'Estimating yield of hardwood coppice for pulpwood growing', *Forestry Commission Report on Forest Research* (HMSO, 1959/60) 189–96

Black, R. F. 'Chestnut coppice with particular reference to layering', *Quarterly Journal of Forestry* (**57**, 1963) 311–19

Blyth, J., Evans, J., Mutch, W. and Sidwell, C. *Farm Woodland Management* (Farming Press, 1987)

Booth, J. C. 'Plantations on medieval rigg and furr cultivation strips', (HMSO, 1967)

Boycott, A. E. 'The habitats of land mollusca in Britain', *Journal of Ecology* (**22**, 1934) 1–38

Bradshaw, R. H. W. 'Spatially precise studies of forest dynamics', in Huntley, B. and Webb, T. (ed) *Vegetation History* (Kluwer, 1988) 727–53

Brandon, P. F. 'Medieval clearances in the East Sussex Weald', *Transactions of the Institute of British Geographers* (**48**, 1969) 135–53

Brasier, C. M. and Webber, J. F. 'Recent advances in Dutch elm disease research: host, pathogen and vector', in Patch, D. (ed) *Advances in Practical Arboriculture* (HMSO, 1987) 166–79

Brooks, A. *Woodlands* (British Trust for Conservation Volunteers, 1988)

Brooks, A. *Dry Stone Walling* (British Trust for Conservation Volunteers, 1983)

Brooks, A. *Hedging* (British Trust for Conservation Volunteers, 1984)

Bunce, R. G. H. *A Field Key for Classifying British Woodland Vegetation* (ITE, 1982)

Bunce, R. G. H. and Jeffers, J. N. R. *Native Pinewoods of Scotland* (ITE, 1977)

Burdekin, D. A. (ed) *Research on Dutch Elm Disease in Europe* (HMSO, 1983)

Cambridge Agrarian History of England and

Wales (Cambridge University Press, 1967 onwards)

Cantor, L. M. and Hatherly, J. 'The medieval parks of England', *Geography* (**64**, 1979) 71–85

Carlisle, A. and Brown, A. H. F. 'The impact of man on the native pinewoods of Scotland', in Bunce, R. G. H. and Jeffers, J. N. R. (ed) *Native Pinewoods of Scotland* (ITE, 1977) 70–7

Chapman, N. and D. *Fallow Deer, Their History, Distribution and Ecology* (Dalton, 1975)

Collins, E. J. T. 'Agriculture and conservation in England: an historical overview', *Journal of the Royal Agricultural Society* (**146**, 1985) 38–46

Collins, E. J. T. 'Changing markets for coppice products and coppice management in England 1750–1914', in Salbitano, F. (ed) *Human Influence on Forest Ecosystems Development in Europe* (Pitagora Editrice Bologna, 1988) 331–4

Collins, M. A. *History and Soils on the South Downs* (King's College, London, 1978)

Cooke, A. (ed) *The Use of Herbicides in Nature Reserves* (Nature Conservancy Council, 1986)

Cooper, A. B. and Mutch, W. 'The management of red deer in plantations', in Ford, E. D., Malcolm, D. C. and Atterson, J. (ed) *The Ecology of Even-aged Plantations* (IUFRO, 1978) 453–62

Coppock, J. T. 'Maps as sources for the study of land use in the past', *Imago Mundi* (**22**, 1968) 37–49

Countryside Commission, *Countryside Management in the Urban Fringe* (Countryside Commission, 1981)

Crowe, S. *Forestry in the Landscape* (HMSO, 1978)

Crowther, R. E. and Evans, J. *Coppice* (HMSO, 1986)

Cummins, R. P. and Miller, G. R. 'Damage by red deer *Cervus elaphus* enclosed in planted woodland', *Scottish Forestry* (**36**, 1982) 1–8

Daniels, S. 'The political iconography of

woodland in late Georgian England', in Cosgrove, D. and Daniels, S. (ed) *The Iconography of the Landscape* (Cambridge University Press, 1988)

Darby, H. C. 'The clearing of the English Woodland', *Geography* (**36**, 1951) 71–83

Darby, H. C. *A New Historical Geography of England after 1600* (Cambridge University Press, 1973)

Darby, H. C. *Domesday England* (Cambridge University Press, 1977)

DART *Small Woods on Farms* (Countryside Commission, 1983)

Dimbleby, G. W. and Gill, J. M. 'The occurrence of podzols under deciduous woodland in the New Forest', *Forestry* (**28**, 1955) 95–106

Directory of British Associations (CBD Research, 1986)

Druce, G. C. 'Botany', in *The Victoria History of the County of Northamptonshire* (Constable, 1902)

Dunlop, B. M. S. 'The regeneration of our native pinewoods', *Scottish Forestry* (**29**, 1975) 111–19

Dunlop, B. M. S. 'The natural regeneration of Scots Pine', *Scottish Forestry* (**37**, 1983) 259–63

Edees, E. S. and Newton, A. *Brambles of the British Isles* (The Ray Society, 1988)

Edlin, H. L. *Forestry and Woodland Life* (Batsford, 1947)

Edwards, I. D. 'The conservation of the Glen Tanar native pinewood, near Arboyne, Aberdeenshire', *Scottish Forestry* (**35**, 1981) 173–79

Edwards, M. E. 'Disturbance histories of four Snowdonian woodlands and their relation to Atlantic Bryophyte distributions', *Biological Conservation* (**37**, 1986) 301–20

Ellenberg, H. *The Vegetation Ecology of Central Europe* (Cambridge University Press, 1988)

Elton, C. *The Pattern of Annim Communities* (Methuen, 1966)

Elwes, H. J. and Henry, A. H. *The Trees of Great Britain and Ireland* (Private, 1906–13)

Emery, M. *Promoting Nature in Cities and Towns. A Practical Guide* (Croom Helm, 1986)

Evans, J. *Silviculture of Broadleaved Woodland* (HMSO, 1984) 115–20

Evans, J. 'The control of epicormic branches', in Patch, D. (ed), *Advances in Practical Arboriculture* (HMSO, 1987) 115–20

Evans, J. *Natural Regeneration of Broadleaves* (HMSO, 1988)

Fairbairn, W. A. 'Dalkeith Old Wood', *Scottish Forestry* (**26**, 1972) 5–28

Faulkner, R. 'The gene-pool of Caledonian Scots pine – its conservation and uses', in Bunce, R. G. H. and Jeffers, J. N. R. (ed) *Native Pinewoods of Scotland* (ITE, 1977) 96–9

Fenton, E. W. 'The oak in Scotland, and two semi-natural oakwoods in the south-east of Scotland', *Forestry* (**15**, 1941) 76–85

Fenton, J. 'Regeneration of native pine in Glen Affric', *Scottish Forestry* (**39**, 1985) 104–16

Fergusson, J. J. 'The census of woodlands – some impressions', *Journal of the Forestry Commission* (**20**, 1949) 54–5

Finberg, H. F. R. *The Early Charters of the West Midlands* (Leicester University Press, 1961, 2nd ed 1972)

Fleming, S. C. 'Problems and possibilities in using large scale twentieth-century maps and aerial photographs to monitor woodland change', in Watkins, C. and Wheeler, P. T. (ed) *The Study and Use of British Woodlands* (University of Nottingham, 1981)

Forestry Commission *Guidelines for the Management of Broadleaved Woodland* (Forestry Commission, 1985)

Forster, J. A. and Morris, D. 'The conservation of the native Scots pinewoods', in Bunce, R. G. H. and Jeffers, J. N. R. *Native Pinewoods of Scotland* (ITE, 1977) 116–120

Frearson, K. and Weiss, N. D. 'Improved growth rates within tree shelters', *Quarterly Journal of Forestry* (**81**, 1987) 184–7

Fuller, R. J. and Warren, M. S. *Coppiced Woodland – Its History, Conservation and Management* (Nature Conservancy Council, in press)

Gelling, M. *Place Names in the Landscape* (Dent, 1984)

Gibson, C. W. D. 'The distribution of "ancient woodland" plant species among areas of different history in Wytham Woods, Oxfordshire', in Kirby, K. J. and Wright, F. J. (ed) *Woodland Conservation and Research in the Clay Vale of Oxfordshire and Buckinghamshire* (Nature Conservancy Council, 1988) 32–40

Gilbert, J. M. *Hunting and Hunting Reserves in Medieval Scotland* (Donald, 1979)

Godwin, H. *History of the British Flora* (Cambridge University Press, 1975)

Goodier, R. and Bunce, R. 'The natural pinewoods of Scotland: the current state of the resource', in Bunce, R. J. H. and Jeffers, J. N. R. (ed) *Native Pinewoods of Scotland* (ITE, 1977) 78–87

Green, F. H. W. 'Ridge and furrow, mole and tile', *Geographical Journal* (**141**, 1975) 88–93

Griffin, N. and Watkins, C. 'Public access to woodlands and the owner's liability as an occupier of land', *Quarterly Journal of Forestry* (**80**, 1986) 151–8

Grigg, D. B. 'The changing agricultural geography of England: a commentary on the sources available for the reconstruction of agriculture', *Transactions of the Institute of British Geographers* (**31**, 1967) 73–96

Grundy, G. B. 'The ancient woodland of Wiltshire', *Wiltshire Archaeological and Natural History Magazine* (**48**, 1939) 530–98

Gurnell, J. *The Natural History of Squirrels* (Christopher Helm, 1987)

Hammersley, G. 'The charcoal iron industry and its fuel', *Economic History Review* (2nd Series **26**, 1973) 593–613

Hammond, B. R. G. 'The suppression of coppice by weeding', *Journal of the Forestry Commission* (**20**, 1949) 112–13

Hanon, G. E. and Bradshaw, R. H. W.

'Recent vegetation dynamics on two Connemara Lake Islands, Western Ireland', *Journal of Biogeography* (**16**, 1989)

Harding, P. T. and Rose, F. *Pasture Woodlands in Lowland Britain* (ITE, 1986)

Harley, J. B. 'The hundred rolls of 1279', *Amateur Historian* (**5**, 1961) 16

Harley, J. B. *The Historian's Guide to Ordnance Survey Maps* (National Council of Social Service, 1964)

Harley, J. B. 'Maps and the local historian: a guide to British sources II: estate maps', *Amateur Historian* (**7**, 1967) 223–31

Harley, J. B. 'County maps', *Local Historian* (**8**, 1969) 167–79

Harley, J. B. *The Ordnance Survey and Land-use Mapping* (Geobooks, 1979)

Harris, L. D. *The Fragmented Forest* (Chicago University Press, 1984)

Harris, L. G. 'Relative growth of coppice from varying number of shoots per stool', *Quarterly Journal of Forestry* (**50**, 1956) 244

Harris, M. J. and Kent, M. 'Ecological benefits of the Bradford-Hutt system of commercial forestry II. The seed bank and the ground flora species phenology', *Quarterly Journal of Forestry* (**81**, 1987) 213–24

Hart, C. E. *Royal Forest: a History of Dean's Woods as Producers of Timber* (Oxford University Press, 1966)

Hedley, W. P. 'The medieval forests of Northumberland', *Archaeologia Aeliana* (**28**, 1950) 96–104

Henderson, C. 'An historical survey of Cornish woodlands', in *Essays in Cornish History* (Oxford, 1935) 135–51

Hendry, G., Bannister, N. and Toms, J. 'The earthworks of an ancient woodland', *Bristol and Avon Archaeology* (**3**, 1984) 47–53

Helliwell, D. R. 'The effects of size and isolation on the conservation value of wooded sites in Britain', *Journal of Biogeography* (**3**, 1976) 407–16

Hibberd, B. G. (ed) *Forestry Practice* (HMSO, 1986)

Hibberd, B. G. (ed) *Farm Woodland Practice* (HMSO, 1988)

Holdsworth, C. J. 'Rufford Charters', Volume 1, *Thoroton Society Record Series* (**29**, 1972)

Holdsworth, C. J. 'Rufford Charters', Volume 2, *Thoroton Society Record Series* (**30**, 1974)

Hooke, D. 'Early Cotswold woodland', *Journal of Historical Geography* (**4**, 1978) 333–41

Hooke, D. *The Anglo-Saxon Landscape of the West Midlands: Charter Evidence* (BAR: **95**, 1981)

Hooke, D. *The Anglo-Saxon Landscape: The Kingdom of the Hwicca* (Manchester University Press, 1985)

Hooke, D. 'Woodland utilisation in England AD800–1100', in Salbitano, F. (ed) *Human Influence on Forest Ecosystems Development in Europe* (Pitagora Editrice Bologna, 1988) 301–10

Hooper, M. D. 'History of Monks Wood', in Steel, R. C. and Welch, R. C. (ed) *Monks Wood: a Nature Reserve Record* (Nature Conservancy, 1973) 22–35

Hornby, R. 'Nature conservation in Chiltern woodlands – a Nature Conservancy Council view', *Quarterly Journal of Forestry* (**31**, 1987) 116–21

Hunter, F. A. 'Ecology of pinewood beetles', in Bunce, R. G. H. and Jeffers, J. N. R. (ed) *Native Pinewoods of Scotland* (ITE, 1977) 42–55

Insley, H. (ed) *Farm Woodland Planning* (HMSO, 1988)

Irving, J. A. *The Public in your Woods* (Packard, 1985)

James, N. D. G. *A History of English Forestry* (Blackwell, 1981)

James, N. D. G. *The Forester's Companion* (Blackwell, 1982)

Jobling, J. and Pearce, M. L. *Free Growth of Oak* (HMSO, 1977)

Jones, E. W. 'The structure and reproduction of the virgin forest of the North Temperate Zone', *New Phytologist*, (**44**, 1945) 130–47

Jones, E. W. 'British Forestry in 1790–1813', *Quarterly Journal of Forestry* (**55**, 1961) 36–40, 131–38

Jones, M. 'Woodland origins in a South Yorkshire parish', *Local Historian* (**16**, 1984) 73–82

Jones, M. *Sheffield's Ancient Woods* (Sheffield Polytechnic, 1986)

Jones, M. and Jones, J. *Sheffield's Historic Woodlands, Past and Present* (Private, 1985)

Kain, R. *An Atlas and Index of the Tithe Files of Mid-nineteenth Century England and Wales* (Cambridge University Press, 1986)

Kain, R. and Prince, H. *The Tithe Surveys of England and Wales* (Cambridge University Press, 1984)

Kenward, R. E., Parish, T., Holm, J. and Harris, E. H. M. 'Grey Squirrel bark stripping – the roles of tree quality, squirrel learning and food abundance', *Quarterly Journal of Forestry* (**82**, 1988) 9–20

Kirby, K. J. *The Control of Bramble in Nature Conservation Areas* (Nature Conservancy Council: CST, Note 16, 1979)

Kirby, K. J. 'Scottish birchwoods and their conservation', *Transactions of the Botanical Society of Edinburgh* (**44**, 1984a) 205–18

Kirby, K. J. *Forestry Operations and Broadleaf Woodland Conservation* (Nature Conservancy Council, 1984b)

Kirby, K. J. *Woodland Survey Handbook* (Nature Conservancy Council, 1988a)

Kirby, K. J. 'Changes in the ground flora under plantations on ancient woodland sites', *Forestry* (**61**, 1988b) 317–38

Kirby, K. J., Bines, T., Burn, A., Mackintosh, J., Pitkin, P. and Smith, I. 'Seasonal and observer differences in vascular plant records from British woodlands', *Journal of Ecology* (**74**, 1986) 123–31

Kirby, K. J., Peterken, G. F., Spencer, J. W. and Walker, G. J. *Inventories of Ancient Semi-natural Woodland* (Nature Conservancy Council, 1984)

Kirby, K. J. and Wright, F. J. (eds) *Woodland Conservation and Research in the Clay Vale of Oxfordshire and Buckinghamshire* (Nature Conservancy Council, 1988)

Koop, H. 'Vegetative reproduction of trees in some European natural forests', *Vegetatio* (**72**, 1987) 103–10

Ley, A. 'Botany', in *The Victoria County History of Herefordshire* (Constable, 1908)

Limbrey, S. *Soil Science and Archaeology* (Academic Press, 1978)

Lindsay, J. M. 'Charcoal iron smelting and its fuel supply: the example of the Lorn Furnace, Argyllshire 1733–1876', *Journal of Historical Geography* (**1**, 1975) 283–98

Linnard, W. 'Forestry in Wales at the Turn of the Eighteenth Century', *Quarterly Journal of Forestry* (**66**, 1972) 208–18

Linnard, W. *Welsh Woods and Forests: History and Utilisation* (National Museum of Wales, 1982)

Linnard, W. 'Sooty bands from tents of turf: wood colliers and charcoal burning in Wales', *Folklife* (**25**, 1987) 47–73

Lloyd, W. F. *Lakeland Charcoal* (Lake District National Park, 1988)

Loudon, J. C. *Arboretum et Fruticetum Britannicum* (Bohn, 1838)

Lowe, R. *General View of the Agriculture of the County of Nottingham* (Nicol, 1798)

MacKintosh, J. *The Woods of Argyll and Bute* (Nature Conservancy Council, 1988)

McIntosh, R. and Henman, D. W. 'Seed fall in the Black Wood of Rannoch', *Scottish Forestry* (**35**, 1981) 249 55

Main, J. *The Forest Planter and Pruner's Assistant* (Ridgway, 1839)

Marren, P. *Woodland Heritage* (David & Charles, 1990)

Marren, P. *Discovering and Exploring Woodland* (David & Charles, 1991)

Mason, C. and Long, S. 'Management of lowland broadleaved woodland, Bovingdon Hall, Essex', in Matthews, R. (ed) *Conservation Monitoring and Management* (Countryside Commission, 1987) 37–42

Mead, W. R. 'Ridge and furrow in Buckinghamshire', *Geographical Journal* (**120**, 1954) 34–42

Miles, J. and Kinnaird, J. W. 'Grazing with particular reference to birch, juniper and Scots pine in the Scottish Highlands', *Scottish Forestry* (**33**, 1979) 280–9

Millman, R. N. *The Making of the Scottish*

Landscape (Batsford, 1975)

Mitchell, B., McCowan, D. and Willcox, N. A. 'Effects of deer in a woodland restoration enclosure', *Scottish Forestry* (**36**, 1982) 102–12

Mitchell, P. and Kirby, K. J. *Ecological Effects of Forestry Practices in Long-established Woodland and their Implications for Nature Conservation* (Oxford Forestry Institute, 1989)

Mitchell, P. 'Re-pollarding large neglected pollards: a review of current practice and results', *Arboricultural Journal* (**13**, 1989)

Monteath, R. *The Forester's Guide and Profitable Planter* (Stirling and Kenney, 1824)

Moody, D. *Scottish Local History* (Batsford, 1986)

Moreno, D. and Montanari, C. 'The use of historical photographs as a source in the study of dynamics of vegetational groups and woodlands landscape', in Salbitano, F. (ed) *Human Influence on Forest Ecosystems Development in Europe* (Pitagora Editrice Bologna, 1988) 371–4

Morgan, R. K. 'An evaluation of the impact of anthropogenic pressure on woodland regeneration in the New Forest, Hampshire', *Biogeography* (**14**, 1987) 439–50

Moseley, S. P. and Moore, P. D. 'The development of forest in south-east England in the last two centuries: evidence from pollen analysis', in Salbitano, F. (ed) *Human Influence on Forest Ecosystems Development in Europe* (Pitagora Editrice Bologna, 1988) 91–4

Muir, R. and Muir, N. *Hedgerows: Their History and Wildlife* (Michael Joseph, 1987)

Nicholls, P. H. 'On the evolution of a forest landscape', *Transactions of the Institute of British Geographers* (**56**, 1972) 57–76

O'Sullivan, P. E. 'Vegetation history and the native pinewoods', in Bunce, R. G. H. and Jeffers, J. N. R. *Native Pinewoods of Scotland* (ITE, 1977)

Ordnance Survey, *Red Book* (Ordnance Survey, 1949)

Ordnance Survey, *Place Names on Maps in Scotland and Wales* (Ordnance Survey, 1987)

Parsons, D. and Evans, J. 'Forest fire protection in the Neath district of South Wales', *Quarterly Journal of Forestry* (**71**, 1977) 186–98

Pepper, H. W. 'Chemical deterrents', (HMSO, 1978)

Pepper, H. W., Rowe, J. and Tee, L. A. *Individual Tree Protection* (HMSO, 1985)

Pepper, H. W. and Tee, L. A. *Forest Fencing* (HMSO, 1986)

Peterken, G. F. 'General management principles for nature conservation in British Woodlands', *Forestry* (**50**, 1977) 27–48

Peterken, G. F. *Woodland Conservation and Management* (Chapman and Hall, 1981)

Peterken, G. F. and Backmeroff, C. *Long-term Monitoring in Unmanaged Woodland Nature Reserves* (Nature Conservancy Council, 1988)

Peterken, G. F. and Game, M. 'Historical factors affecting the distribution of *Mercurialis perennis* in central Lincolnshire', *Journal of Ecology* (**69**, 1981) 781–96

Peterken, G. F. and Game, M. 'Historical factors affecting the number and distribution of vascular plant species in the woodlands of central Lincolnshire', *Journal of Ecology* (**72**, 1984) 155–82

Peterken, G. F. and Jones, E. W. 'Forty years of change in Lady Park Wood: the old growth stands', *Journal of Ecology* (**75**, 1987) 477–512

Peterken, G. F. and Jones, E. W. 'Forty years of change in Lady Park Wood: the young growth stands', *Journal of Ecology* (**77**, 1989)

Peterken, G. F. and Stace, H. 'Stand development in the Black Wood of Rannoch', *Scottish Forestry* (**41**, 1987) 29–44

Peterken, G. F. and Tubbs, C. R. 'Woodland regeneration in the New Forest, Hampshire, since 1650', *Journal of Applied Ecology* (**2**, 1965) 159–70

Phillips, J. B. 'Effect of cutting techniques on coppice regrowth', *Quarterly Journal of Forestry* (**65**, 1971) 220–3

Pigott, C. D. 'Regeneration of oak-birch woodland following exclusion of sheep', *Journal of Ecology* (**71**, 1983) 629–46

Pollard, E., Hooper, M. D. and Moore, N. W. *Hedges* (Collins, 1974)

Pott, R. 'Impact of human influences by extensive woodland management and former land use in north-western Europe', in Salbitano, F. (ed) *Human Influence on Forest Ecosystems Development in Europe* (Pitagora Editrice Bologna, 1988) 263–78

Potter, M. 'Shelters: questions and answers', *Forestry and British Timber* (**16**, No 11, 1987) 28–9

Price, U. *Essays on the Picturesque, as Compared with the Sublime and the Beautiful . . .* (Mawman, 1810)

Prior, R. *The Roe Deer of Cranborne Chase: An Ecological Study* (Oxford University Press, 1968)

Prior, R. *Trees and Deer* (Batsford, 1983)

Prior, R. *Deer Management in Small Woodlands* (Game Conservancy, 1987)

Proctor, M. C. F., Spooner, G. M. and Spooner, M. F. 'Changes in Wistman's Wood, Dartmoor: photographic and other evidence', *Reports and Transactions of the Devonshire Association for the Advancement of Science* (**112**, 1980) 43–79

Pryor, S. N. and Savill, P. S. *Silvicultural Systems for Broadleaved Woodland in Britain* (Oxford Forestry Institute Occasional Paper No 32, 1986)

Pugh, R. B. *The Victoria History of the Counties of England: General Introduction* (Oxford University Press, 1970)

Putman, R. *Grazing in Temperate Ecosystems: Large Herbivores and the Ecology of the New Forest* (Croom Helm, 1986)

Rackham, O. (ed) *Hayley Wood: Its History and Ecology* (Cambridge and Isle of Ely Naturalists Trust, 1975)

Rackham, O. *Trees and Woodland in the British Landscape* (Dent, 1976)

Rackham, O. *Ancient Woodland: Its History, Vegetation and Uses in England* (Edward Arnold, 1980)

Rackham, O. *The History of the British Countryside* (Dent, 1986a)

Rackham, O. *The Ancient Woods of England: Woods of SE Essex* (Rochford District Council, 1986b)

Rackham, O. *The Last Forest: The Story of Hatfield Forest* (Dent, 1989)

Ratcliffe, D. A. 'An ecological account of Atlantic bryophytes in the British Isles', *New Phytologist* (**67**, 1968) 365–439

Reed, T. *Management Plans* (Nature Conservancy Council, 1988)

Reid, C. *The Origin of the British Flora* (Dulan, 1899)

Riden, P. *Local History: A Handbook for Beginners* (Batsford, 1983)

Riden, P. *Record Sources for Local History* (Batsford, 1987)

Robertson, P., Woodburn, M. and Hill, D. 'The effects of woodland management for pheasants on the abundance of butterflies in Dorset', *Biological Conservation* (**45**, 1988) 159–67

Robinson, S. 'The forests and woodlands of Herefordshire', *Transactions of the Woolhope Naturalists Field Club* (1925) 193–220

Roden, D. 'Woodland and its management in the medieval Chilterns', *Forestry* (**41**, 1968) 59–71

Rodger, E. M. *The Large Scale County Maps of the British Isles 1596–1850* (Bodleian Library, 1972)

Rodwell, J. *British Plant Communities* (Cambridge University Press, in press)

Rollinson, T. *Thinning Control* (HMSO, 1985)

Rollinson, T. and Evans, J. *The Yield of Sweet Chestnut Coppice* (HMSO, 1987)

Rose, F. 'Lichenological indicators of age and environmental continuity in woodlands', in Brown, D., Hawkesworth, D. and Bailey, R. (ed) *Lichenology: Progress and Problems* (Academic Press, 1976) 279–307

Rowe, J. *Badger Gates* (HMSO, 1976)

Rowe, J. *Grey Squirrel Control* (HMSO, 1980)

Salbitano, F. (ed) *Human Influence on Forest Ecosystems Development in Europe* (Pitagora Editrice Bologna, 1988)

Salisbury, E. J. and Tansley, A. G. 'The durmast oakwoods (*Querceta sessiflorae*) of the Silurian and Malvernian strata near Malvern', *Journal of Ecology* (**9**, 1922) 19–38

Savill, P. and Evans, J. *Plantation Silviculture in Temperate Regions* (Clarendon Press, 1986)

Sawyer, P. H. *Anglo-Saxon Charters: An Annotated List and Bibliography* (Royal Historical Society, 1968)

Schlich, W. *Forestry in the UK* (Bradbury Agnew, 1904)

Seymour, S. *Eighteenth-century Parkland 'improvement' on the Dukeries' Estates of North Nottinghamshire*, Unpublished PhD Thesis (University of Nottingham, 1988)

Shaw, G. and Tipper, A. *British Directories* (Leicester University Press, 1989)

Shaw, M. W. '*Rhododendron ponticum*: ecological reasons for the success of an alien species in Britain and features that may assist its control', *Aspects of Applied Biology* (**5**, 1984) 231–53

Sheail, J. *Historical Ecology: The Documentary Evidence* (ITE, 1980)

Sheail, J. *Rural Conservation in Inter-war Britain* (Oxford University Press, 1981)

Silvanus, *Information Sheet One* (Silvanus, 1987)

Smart, N. and Andrews, J. *Birds and Broadleaves Handbook* (Royal Society for the Protection of Birds, 1985)

Soutar, R. G. and Peterken, G. F. 'Regional lists of native trees and shrubs for use in afforestation schemes', *Arboricultural Journal* (**13**, 1989) 33–43

Stamp, L. D. *The Land of Britain – Its Use and Misuse* (Longmans, 1948)

Steele, R. and Peterken, G. F. 'Management objectives for broadleaved woodland conservation', in Malcolm, D. C., Evans, J. and Edwards, P. N. (ed) *Broadleaves in Britain* (Institute of Chartered Foresters, 1982) 91–103

Steele, R. and Welch, R. C. (ed) *Monks Wood* (Nature Conservancy, 1973)

Stephens, W. B. *Sources for English Local History* (Manchester University Press, 1981)

Sterling, P. H. and Hambler, C. 'Coppicing for conservation: do hazel communities benefit?', in Kirby, K. J. and Wright F. J. (ed) *Woodland Conservation and Research in the Clay Vale of Oxfordshire and Buckinghamshire* (Nature Conservancy Council, 1988) 69–80

Steven, H. M. and Carlisle, A. *The Native Pinewoods of Scotland* (Oliver and Boyd, 1959)

Symon, J. A. *Scottish Farming: Past and Present* (Oliver and Boyd, 1959)

Tabbush, P. M. and Williamson, D. R. *Rhododendron ponticum as a Forest Weed* (HMSO, 1987)

Tansley, A. G. *The British Islands and their Vegetation* (Cambridge University Press, 1939)

Tate, W. E. (ed M. E. Turner) *A Domesday of English Enclosure Acts and Awards* (Reading University Library Publications, 1978)

Taylor, R. W. 'The sycamore *Acer pseudoplatanus* in Britain – its natural history and value to wildlife', *Discussion Papers in Conservation* (**42**, 1985)

Taylor, R. *George Washington Wilson: Artist and Photographer 1823–93* (Aberdeen University Press, 1982)

Thomas, K. *Man and the Natural World* (Allen Lane, 1983)

Tilney-Bassett, H. A. 'Forestry in the region of the Chilterns', *Forestry* (**61**, 1988) 267–86

Timson, R. T. 'The Cartulary of Blyth Priory', *Thoroton Society Record Series* (**27**, 1973)

Tittensor, R. M. 'History of the Loch Lomond Oakwoods', *Scottish Forestry* (**24**, 1970) 101–18

Tittensor, R. M. 'The history of the Mens: a Sussex woodland common', *Sussex Archaeological Collections* (**116**, 1978) 347–74

Townsend, M. G., Bunyan, P. J., Odam, E. M., Stanley, P. I., Wardall, H. P. 'Assessment of secondary poisoning hazard of Warfarin to least-weasels', *Journal of Wildlife Management* (**48**, 1984) 628–35

Troup, R. S. *Silvicultural Systems* (Oxford University Press, 1928)

Tubbs, C. R. *The New Forest: An Ecological History* (David & Charles, 1968)

Tubbs, C. R. *The New Forest* (Collins, 1986)

Turner, M. E. *English Parliamentary Enclosure* (Dawson, 1980)

Upex, S. *The Reconstruction of Open Field Layout from Landscape Evidence in Northamptonshire and Cambridgeshire*, Unpublished PhD Thesis (University of Nottingham, 1984)

Walker, G. and Kirby, K. 'An historical approach to woodland conservation in Scotland', *Scottish Forestry* (**41**, 1987)

Waring, P. 'Responses of moth populations to coppicing and the planting of conifers', in Kirby, K. J. and Wright, F. J. (ed) *Woodland Conservation and Research in the Clay Vale of Oxfordshire and Buckinghamshire* (Nature Conservancy Council, 1988) 82–113

Warren, M. S. 'The status of heath fritillary butterfly *Mellicta athalia* Rott. in relation to changing woodland management in the Blean Woods, Kent', *Quarterly Journal of Forestry* (**79**, 1985) 175–82

Warren, M. S. and Fuller, R. J. *The Management of Woodland Rides and Glades for Wildlife* (Nature Conservancy Council, in press)

Watkins, C. 'An historical introduction to the woodlands of Nottinghamshire', in Watkins, C. and Wheeler, P. T. (ed) *The Study and Use of British Woodlands* (University of Nottingham, 1981) 1–24

Watkins, C. 'The use of Forestry Commission censuses for the study of woodland change', *Journal of Historical Geography* (**10**, 1984a) 396–406

Watkins, C. 'Woodland clearance in England and Wales', *Arboricultural Journal* (**8**, 1984b) 299–315

Watkins, C. 'The planting of woodland in Nottinghamshire since 1945', *East Midland Geographer* (**8**, 1984c) 147–58

Watkins, C. 'Sources for the assessment of British woodland change', *Applied Geography* (**5**, 1985) 153–68

Watkins, C. 'The future of woodlands in the rural landscape', in Lockart, D. and Ilberry, B. (ed) *The Future of the British Rural Landscape* (Geobooks, 1987) 71–96

Watkins, C. 'The idea of ancient woodland in Britain from 1800', in Salbitano, F. (ed) *Human Influence on Forest Ecosystems Development in Europe* (Pitagora Editrice Bologna, 1988) 237–46

Watson, A. 'Eighteenth Century deer numbers and pine regeneration near Braemar', *Biological Conservation* (**25**, 1983) 287–305

Watt, A. S. 'On the ecology of British beechwoods with special reference to their regeneration', *Journal of Ecology* (**11**, 1923) 1–48

Watt, T. A., Kirby, K. J. and Savill, P. J. 'Effects of herbicides on woodland plant communities', *Aspects of Applied Biology* (**16**, 1988) 383–92

Way, L. 'An account of the Leigh Woods in the parish of Ashton, County of Somerset', *Transactions of the Bristol and Gloucestershire Archaeological Society* (**36**, 1913) 55–102

West, J. *Remarks on the Management or Rather the Mis-management of Woods, Plantations and Hedgerow Timber* (Longman and Co, 1842)

Wheeler, P. T. 'A survey of woodland change in Nottinghamshire, 1920–1980', *East Midland Geographer* (**8**, 1984) 134–47

Whitehead, G. K. *The Deer of Great Britain and Ireland* (Routledge, 1964)

Whittington, G. and Gibson, A. *The Military Survey of Scotland 1747–1755: A Critique* (Geobooks, 1986)

Whyte, I. D. and Whyte, K. A. *Sources for Scottish Historical Geography: An Introductory Guide* (Geobooks, 1981)

Wildgoose, M. 'Roystone Grange', *Current Archaeology* (**9**, 1987) 303–7

Williams, M. *The Draining of the Somerset Levels* (Cambridge University Press, 1970)

Willmott, K. J. *The Ecology and Conservation of the Purple Emperor Butterfly* Apatura iris (World Wildlife Fund, 1987)

Woodland Trust. *Community Woodland Resource Pack* (Woodland Trust, 1986)

Young, C. R. *The Royal Forests of Medieval England* (Leicester University Press, 1979)

Acknowledgements

I have received help and assistance from many people. I would particularly like to thank George Peterken, Keith Kirby and Jonathan Spencer without whose help and guidance this book would not have been written; Peter Wakely, who took most of the photographs; and John Peters and Martin Timms of Esso UK plc.

The staff of the Nature Conservancy Council have been very helpful. Shirley Penny, Malcolm Rush and the other library staff at the Nature Conservancy Council were always ready to provide invaluable assistance. I would also like to thank Philip Oswald, Tony Whitbread, Rob Cooke, Amanda Giles, Sarah Webster, Arnie Cook, Terry Rowell, Rosie Carmichael, Dick Hornby, Peter Marren and many other people on the staff of the Nature Conservancy Council.

I would like to thank the following people who provided essential information, or made valuable comments on various sections: Norman Lewis of the Nottinghamshire Trust for Nature Conservation; John Sheail of the Institute of Terrestrial Ecology; Charles Couzens of the RSNC; David Postle; Elizabeth Hamilton; Roger Kain of the Department of Geography, University of Exeter; Bill Linnard; Ted Collins of the Museum of English Rural Life, University of Reading; Melvyn Jones of Sheffield Polytechnic; Stephen Upex of Peterborough College; Oliver Rackham of Corpus Christi College, Cambridge; Charles Withers of the College of St Paul and St Mary, Cheltenham; Della Hooke of the Department of Geography, University of Birmingham; Paul Tiplady of Essex County Council and Peter Mitchell of the School of Botany, University of Cambridge. I would like to thank the archivists at various County Record Offices for allowing me to reproduce documents in their care, the many woodland owners who have allowed me to visit their woods, and my colleagues at the Royal Agricultural College, Cirencester, for their help and encouragement.

Index

Page numbers in *italics* indicate illustrations